11-14

How to REALLY Pay "Wholesale" for College
Andrew Lockwood, CollegeSuccessBulletin.com

How to Pay "Wholesale" for College

Andrew Lockwood, J.D.

Disclaimer

(To prove that I went to law school)

To make this book even more gripping, I decided to start off with a nice, weasel-like disclaimer so some idiot doesn't sue me.

I have made every effort to make this book the best book on this topic in the history of mankind, but there is a distinct possibility that I made one or a few mistakes, such as typographical errors, or even in the content, such as inadvertent admissions or summaries of complicated rules (that you wouldn't want to read anyway).

So please consider this book as a general guide and consult a qualified advisor if you have any questions about your specific situation.

This book is not legal, financial or any other advice. And you should not rely on the examples of successful clients described herein. Just because they got great results, doesn't mean that you will. Your results could be equal, worse, or better.

I, my advisors and anyone else who contributed to this book, are in no way liable or responsible to you or any person for any damage or liability caused directly or indirectly by information in this book.

So there.

Lockwood College Consulting
497 South Oyster Bay Road
Plainview, New York 11803

Telephone: 516.882.5464
AndyLockwood.com

Printed in the U.S.A

TABLE OF CONTENTS

When "Mr. Wrong" can turn into "Mr. Right"

INTRODUCTION

I wrote this book for the money.

No, I did not receive a seven-figure advance…I'm not part of the *Keeping Up With the College Planners* cast!

Although my original version of *How to Pay "Wholesale" for College* sold a couple hundred more copies than anticipated[1], I wasn't writing it to make money off you.

Nope, I did it so YOU could make money – from the rip-off, overpriced colleges. By avoiding needlessly paying "sticker" price.

Only suckers pay retail!

A lot has changed in the last two years since publication, although *Plus ca change, plus c'est la meme chose (*the more things change, the more they say the same):[2]

College costs continue to skyrocket;

The economy still sucks; and

---

[1] i.e., a couple hundred copies total.

[2] One of the three things I learned from five years of French. (Fine, I looked it up online.)

How to REALLY Pay "Wholesale" for College
Andrew Lockwood, CollegeSuccessBulletin.com

College is harder to get into than ever.

Congress and the present administration have taken baby steps to address the first and second issues, but who knows what will happen with the last one (or any of them, for that matter)?

What you'll get out of this book

I'm going to lay out the actual, tested and proven tactics I use in my practice to help parents – particularly "Forgotten Middle Class" families — who think they can't qualify for any financial aid – cut their college costs by 25%, 33%, 50% or more. They're all here, I have no interest in holding anything back.

Who is this book for?

This book is for:

Six and even seven-figure earning families

Lawyers, Doctors, Dentists, Accountants, Financial Advisors and other professionals

Business Owners

Divorced or separated families

Concerned guidance counselors, educators and administrators who want to help families under their charge.

Anyone confused and stressed about how the hell THEY can possibly afford to send their kids to college.

Warning

I tried to make this book a little funny (not easy, considering the subject matter). My sense of humor has been described as "puerile," "offensive," and "idiotic…" and that's just my mom!

Please do not take my irreverent[3] tone to mean that I'm making light of your situation. But if you can't take a little goof once in a while, maybe you should stop reading now.

Instead, please realize that I wrote this way to help you loosen up, chill out and free up your mind to the possibilities that you CAN obtain relief![4]

OK, enough chit-chat – let's go!

---

[3] That's a nicer word
[4] And because I wanted to write something that I could stomach reading!

CHAPTER 1

HOW DOES IT ALL WORK, ANYWAY?

Here is a two-minute drill explanation on how the whole financial aid process works. Because this is a summary, I am leaving a handful of less-important details out. But I'll cover the important missing stuff in the rest of this book.

What is "Financial Aid?"

Many parents think the term "Financial Aid" refers to loans, only. It doesn't.

"Financial Aid" is a catch-all term that includes loans, work-study, and free stuff – grants and scholarships.

"Grants" usually refer to free money awarded based on "Financial Need," i.e. "how you look on paper based on income, assets, number of kids in college at the time, age and other factors.

"Scholarships" typically indicate merit-based awards, meaning money given for grades, scores, athletic ability, performing arts talent and so forth. (You'll see that many colleges use the term

How to REALLY Pay "Wholesale" for College
Andrew Lockwood, CollegeSuccessBulletin.com

"Merit" loosely – they award money to non-academically elite, non-athletes and non-performing artists too.)

One applicant can receive a wide range of awards from each of the colleges she applies to.

How Do You Apply for Financial Aid?

You apply by filling out forms and submitting them to the schools your child is applying to. Most people do this online, but I suppose some schools still accept hard copies.[5] The forms are:

The Free Application for Federal Student Aid, or FAFSA. The Federal form, required by all colleges. It's free.[6]

The FAFSA is a little more than 100 questions, asking mostly about income, savings accounts and other tedious stuff.

The directions are clear for the most part, but I see mistakes all the time. I point out some of the biggies in a later chapter, but if you want a visual walk-through of where the deadliest, money-losing mistakes lurk on the FAFSA, watch our webinar at www.iLoveFAFSA.com.

The CSS Financial Aid Profile (we in the biz call it "The Profile" or the "CSS Profile"[7]) is another popular, but far less common form,

---

[5] Please submit them online, even if you have to drive your horse and buggy to a local library. This is how colleges want the forms, and this Internet thing is here to stay. ☺

[6] Yeah, I know you can read, but sometimes people go to another site, FAFSA.com, which some genius snapped up so he could charge people to do their financial aid forms (FAFSA.gov is the official site for the free form).

How to REALLY Pay "Wholesale" for College
Andrew Lockwood, CollegeSuccessBulletin.com

used by roughly 250 colleges, typically private schools with their own endowment money to dole out, instead of only Federal grants and loans.

The Profile is a pain in the rumpus! It's more than 200 questions, and much more detailed than the FAFSA.

Why so cumbersome? My guess is that colleges with their own institutional endowment funds want more detail on your financial picture before they decide to commit them. So they rake you over the coals, with all sorts of detailed questions not on the FAFSA, such as:

The value of your retirement accounts

The fair market value of your home

Your mortgage balances and monthly payments

The year you bought your home and price paid

How much you can afford to pay for college

Whether you anticipate help from any other family members or other sources to help you pay for college

Profit and Loss, Balance Sheet and other information about your business, if self-employed

---

[7] "CSS" stands for "College Scholarship Search." Who cares? I do, but not that much – it took me about three years in this business before I bothered to look it up.

How to REALLY Pay "Wholesale" for College
Andrew Lockwood, CollegeSuccessBulletin.com

Whether you have savings in any of your OTHER kids' names

More!

Here's the kicker: your STUDENT is supposed to fill out the Profile!

You read that correctly. The CSS Profile is made by the College Board – the same College Board that administers the SAT.

When your child registers for the PSAT, in Sophomore or Junior year, she creates a College Board user name and password. These login credentials are the same used to access the CSS Profile.

Here's some savvy advice from a high-priced college finance consultant (*Moi*):

Do NOT let your child fill out your financial aid forms!

(Unless you're comfortable turning over your tax returns, bank statements, etc. to young Jared and trusting him to understand them.)

RESOURCE: I cover the entire financial aid process, soup-to-nuts, including key differences of the FAFSA and CSS Profile, in a free online workshop (that I no longer conduct live). Check it out at: Wholesale4College.com/online-workshop.

If you are a business owner whose child is applying to a school that takes the CSS Profile[8], you'll likely be required to complete and submit a Business/Farm Supplement, which consists of basic financial information that your accountant can handwrite.

<u>Supplemental Forms</u>

A small number of colleges require you to fill out their own, unique forms. Check with each college.

When Do You Apply for Financial Aid?

You apply BEFORE you know whether or not your child got into the colleges on his or her list. In other words, you apply to "purchase" your product – a degree – before you know how much it will cost.[9]

Most high school seniors submit their ADMISSIONS applications sometime in the fall, say October or November.

Most FINANCIAL AID applications are submitted in January or February, in accordance with each college's financial aid Priority Deadlines.[10]

---

[8] Always check with each college on your list what forms it requires. Here's a link to a list of all CSS Profile schools published by the College Board: https://profileonline.collegeboard.org/prf/PXRemotePartInstitutionServlet/PXRemotePartInstitutionServlet.srv

[9] Can you imagine buying a car or a home this way? Or paying a fee, spending hours and countless dollars primping and preening (taking tests and prep. courses) to look good ("apply") to the seller of a car or home?

[10] Typically February 15th or March 1, but this is important to research on each school's website because Priority Deadlines vary.

Note that this is long before you'll file your tax returns. How do you pull this off?

You use estimated income on the financial aid forms, then amend the forms once you have actual numbers[11].

This is important – and highlights a key mistake that MANY families make. Don't delay filing your financial aid forms until after you've completed your taxes! File with estimates, amend later.

Yes, there are exceptions. If your child applies Early Decision or Early Action, the deadlines for those applications sometimes coincide with the deadline for one of the financial aid forms required by many competitive colleges – the aforementioned CSS Profile. Early CSS Profile application deadlines could be November 1 or November 15. Be sure to research this if you're applying Early Action or Early Decision.

For the most part, the CSS Profile and FAFSA, are submitted after the first of the year (you cannot submit a FAFSA before January 1 of the year you want financial aid).

Note: returning students have Priority Deadlines later than 1st year students, for the most part. Check your college's website.[12]

---

[11] Using either a service called IDOC – used by most – not all - colleges requiring the CSS Profile – or the IRS Data Retrieval Tool, which the financial aid office will request you to do. (It's really too boring to explain here, just know that the college will tell you what to do!) If you can't get figure out these tools, most schools will accept signed, hard copy tax returns. But check with them!
[12] I'm such a broken record!

How to REALLY Pay "Wholesale" for College
Andrew Lockwood, CollegeSuccessBulletin.com

What will you get?

How do colleges determine how much aid you'll qualify for? There are 70-plus (I've heard 77 but haven't bothered to count) factors that make up the key calculation in the financial aid formulas – the Estimated Family Contribution (EFC).

Income is the most heavily weighted factor – penalized between 22-47% (I explain this later).

Assets are another – child assets are treated differently than parent assets (20% penalty versus 5.64%).

But these are not the only elements that can affect how much you'll have to pay for college. Here are a handful of other considerations:

Your age

The number of students in college at the same time

Whether you own a business

Your marital status[13]

Things that have nothing to do with you, such as the historical generosity of the college

So just because you earn a decent income – or what you assume is a high income – you should not blow off applying for financial aid. Income is but one of many factors.

---

[13] Meaning single or married, not "happy" or "I tolerate my husband."

How to REALLY Pay "Wholesale" for College
Andrew Lockwood, CollegeSuccessBulletin.com

OK, so the financial aid applications are submitted in the beginning of the year. By March, your child will have heard back from all colleges she applied to, whether admitted or not.

A few weeks later, typically by the end of March, you will receive a financial aid award letter from each college your child has been admitted to.

What happens if you're not happy with the award? You can try to improve it, because it's not a firm, take it or leave it, written in stone award. It's only an OFFER.

You can try to improve your financial aid award letter – I cover this "Appeal" process in a later chapter. (Also, I offer a class on all possible techniques you can use to improve a less-than-generous financial aid offer: www.AppealsClass.com.)

Next, the dust settles, your child picks the college she'll attend and you're (moderately) happy with your financial aid award. Summer comes and goes and your child heads off to college. Are you through with the financial aid process?

Unfortunately, your sneaking suspicion is correct – you have to re-file the next year. And the next.

Why must you suffer like Bill Murray in "Groundhog Day?"

Because circumstances change year to year– people lose jobs, make more money, come into inheritances and so forth. Colleges want to know about your financial status each year. If

How to REALLY Pay "Wholesale" for College
Andrew Lockwood, CollegeSuccessBulletin.com

there's a significant change, they'll want to know why. So a change in circumstances can work for or against you.

Still with me?[14] That's the financial aid process in a nutshell.

Now let's get into the details of how to play the financial aid game and win!

---

[14] Still awake?

How to REALLY Pay "Wholesale" for College
Andrew Lockwood, CollegeSuccessBulletin.com

How to REALLY Pay "Wholesale" for College
Andrew Lockwood, CollegeSuccessBulletin.com

CHAPTER 2

COLLEGE TUITION IS "TOO DAMN HIGH!"
How can this be legal?

In 2010, a mutton-chopped guy – I forget his name and don't feel like looking it up – ran for Governor of the State of New York under the auspices of the "Rent is Too Damn High" Party.

Muttonchops cracked me up, but he had a point, easily transferrable to the world of college costs: Tuition is too damn high! The odds are stacked against the average family.

I'm about to share something that stunned even me.[15] I'll let the numbers speak for themselves – annual tuition charged by top private colleges:

Dartmouth:	$37,250
NYU:	$37,372
Barnard:	$37,538

---

[15] Yes, me, perennial winner of the "Most Cynical College Planner" title.

15
How to REALLY Pay "Wholesale" for College
Andrew Lockwood, CollegeSuccessBulletin.com

Haverford:	$37,525
Penn:	$37,376
U Chicago:	$37,632
Williams:	$37,640
Mount Holyoke:	$37,646
Etc. Etc. Etc.	

Gee, do you think anything funny is going on there?

When I came across this data in the book *Higher Education?*[16] It conjured up images of good ol' Teddy Roosevelt busting up John D. Rockefeller's Standard Oil, because trusts were non-competitive and led to higher prices for consumers.

So how is it that each of these schools (including U Chicago, one of the first Rockefeller-funded colleges) charges almost exactly the same tuition? Why do NYU and Dartmouth bill the same amount – it's not like the cost of living in New York City is close to that in to rural New Hampshire!

College costs increase ALL the time – roughly double the rate of inflation[17]. College costs go up in good economies (remember those?) and bad economies.

---

[16] Hacker and Dreifus, 2010, Henry Holt & Company LLC. If you want updated numbers, they're easily found online, but you could also just add $8,000 to each of these figures and call it a day.

[17] 1,000% in the last 30 years, vs. 300% inflation in the same period.

Tuition and fees increase at roughly double the rate of inflation, and faster than every other benchmark, even health care costs.

No – something else is going on here.

Colleges are BUSINESSES (gasp!).

Like any business, they have costs. And they must market themselves[18] to attract paying customers – what you and I call "college students."

Their goal – to get as much money out of your pockets as possible.

You, of course, have the opposite goal – to spend as little as possible, perhaps doing something completely nuts like retiring someday, or paying off the mortgage.

If your child is shooting for a competitive college, but you're freaked out by these numbers (which do NOT include annual room and board, fees and other amounts totaling roughly $15,000 per school), I want you to know that the average discount given by a private college or university is 45%. (Feel better yet? A little?)

Enough about you and your problems. ☺

---

[18] Check your mailbox – ever wonder why you get dozens of pieces of direct mail from colleges you never heard of each week?

How to REALLY Pay "Wholesale" for College
Andrew Lockwood, CollegeSuccessBulletin.com

How are colleges doing, anyway? Has the recession hurt their ability to give out financial aid? Let's look at their bank accounts.

How to REALLY Pay "Wholesale" for College
Andrew Lockwood, CollegeSuccessBulletin.com

CHAPTER 3

COLLEGE ENDOWMENTS
Not too shabby!

I find it irritating[19] when colleges claim that they don't have enough in the budget to award to students who need it. Just like people, they have a way of coming up with money for things (students) they want.

Let's take a look at endowment performance.

College endowments may be down in Fiscal Year 2012, according to the National Association of College and University Business Officers.

But in 2011, they posted returns averaging 19%!

And 10.2% over three years, and more than 6% over the last 10.

---

[19] Then again, I'm easily irritated.

How to REALLY Pay "Wholesale" for College
Andrew Lockwood, CollegeSuccessBulletin.com

According to the NACUBO[20], colleges with the largest endowments, Yale, Harvard and other schools you could probably name, did the best. Nice comeback from 2008, right? And not too bad overall, considering that this 10 year period included our financial meltdown.

True, their costs are up, so no college has an unlimited amount of funds to award. But what are they spending on?

---

[20] Yeah, I used "NACUBO" in a sentence, like it's an everyday term like "CEO." I'm going to find a place in this book to seamlessly integrate another of my faves, "NESCAC."

CHAPTER 4

YOU SHOULDN'T COUNT ON THE FINANCIAL AID OFFICE, YOUR GUIDANCE COUNSELOR OR YOUR ACCOUNTANT FOR HELP...

...unless you like banging your head against a brick wall.

You've got a better shot of running into Paris Hilton at your next MENSA meeting than getting meaningful help from your friendly financial aid officer.

The reason is related to the nature of higher educational institutions themselves – they are BUSINESSES. [21]

Yes, I know that colleges are ivory-towered *institutions of higher education*. However, they have bills to pay too, like any business. Here are a few line items on most schools' budgets:

"Deep" six or even seven figure salaries to pay to university presidents and other higher ups. And not only for colleges you've

---

[21] Oh no he didn't!

heard of, the president of Mountain State University earned $1.8 Million in 2009 (he was fired in 2012).

Many colleges employ *marketing personnel* to help them raise their profile and attract applicants. They don't come cheap: Purdue's Chief Marketing Officer earns "between $200,000-$400,000.[22]

Upgrades to their already luxurious health facilities. Hey, you're slumming it if you don't have a rock climbing wall or "lazy river" for students to enjoy![23]

Dining options such as skirt steak, sushi, vegan, gluten-free and other fare required by today's teens. No more "Bug Juice" or "Mystery Meat."

Full-time wages for tenured professors who teach a grueling two classes per semester, which interferes with their research and publication of dry academic materials that no-one – even other academic types-will read.

Irony alert: Elizabeth Warren, new Senator from Massachusetts and a self-described champion of college cost reform, taught one class at Harvard Law School in Fall 2011.

Her salary: $350,000.

---

[22] Source: http://online.wsj.com/article/SB100008723963904442331045775911716867097 92.html
[23] I wish I were exaggerating. Have you toured a campus lately?

Colleges are spending more on administrative staff than ever. According to a *Bloomberg* article, colleges employed 230,000 administrative staffers in 2009, up 60% since 1993, or 10 times the growth of teaching faculty.

The University of Connecticut's chief of police pulls in $256,000 per annum, more than New York City's police commissioner.

Also:

> UConn has a $312,000-a-year provost and 13 vice, deputy and associate vice provosts, including one overseeing "engagement" who makes almost $275,000 a year. The university has seven vice presidents and 13 deans. President Susan Herbst, who receives a $500,000 salary, has a $199,000 chief of staff.[24]

Don't ask a financial aid officer – an employee of this business – how to shave a few donuts off your bill. Asking the financial office for help is like calling the IRS and demanding that they reveal all their latest loopholes so you can lower your tax bill!

A quick note on other traditional sources of advice:

High School guidance counselors: quality varies, just like doctors, lawyers and hair dressers. They can be great, they can be

---

[24] Source: Bloomberg.com, Bureaucrats Paid $250,000 Feed Outcry Over College Costs, November 14, 2012

How to REALLY Pay "Wholesale" for College
Andrew Lockwood, CollegeSuccessBulletin.com

horrible (Note to any guidance counselors reading this – no, you're not one of the horrible ones).

It's highly unusual to find a guidance counselor or college advisor, from a public or private high school, who understands the nuances buried in the 1,100-plus pages of the Title IV Federal Financial Aid regulations – which assets count against you more than others, which don't count against you at all, that kind of thing.

Parents complain how disappointed they are at their school's lack of financial guidance, but I think the problem is that they have unreasonable expectations. Guidance counselors aren't trained for this type of specialized knowledge, so it's unfair to expect them to have this expertise.

Not to mention their case load – at many public schools one guidance counselor is in charge of 200-400 students, often more. A huge portion of their days is spent on endless meetings and other administrative tasks, dealing with truancies, drug use, bullying, cyber-bullying and other problems that your child may not have, but comprise high school life today. Point is; there's not a ton of time left over for individualized college advice, let alone mastering college financial planning.

Ditto for financial folks: CPA's, CFP's and other advisors rarely have more than a cursory understanding of the financial aid regulations, if they have any. Actually, they frequently give advice that can flat-out *slaughter* your chances of qualifying for anything.

How to REALLY Pay "Wholesale" for College
Andrew Lockwood, CollegeSuccessBulletin.com

A common example: putting money in your child's name may help defer or reduce taxes (since earnings will be taxed at your child's lower rate) - but the financial aid formulas penalize child assets about four times as heavily as parent assets (20% versus 5.64%)!

Be careful whom you listen to. By the time you make it through the end of this book,[25] I bet you'll know more about financial aid than 99% of guidance counselors, accountants and other financial advisors.

---

[25] After you doze off 2-3 times

How to REALLY Pay "Wholesale" for College
Andrew Lockwood, CollegeSuccessBulletin.com

How to REALLY Pay "Wholesale" for College
Andrew Lockwood, CollegeSuccessBulletin.com

CHAPTER 5

THE FINANCIAL AID "GAME" AND HOW TO WIN IT

Two near identical families. One does wicked awesome!

The other...not so much

If you're like most parents of college-bound teens, you have a decent idea about how much college costs...but you're in the dark about how the financial aid "game" is played.

Maybe you've heard rumors of an apparently well-off family getting "a 100% free ride" for their kid, who wasn't an academic or athletic superstar.

How did they do this (putting aside the improbability that they actually received 100% funding)? It's possible that they were able to pay "wholesale" rates for college because they had the scuttlebutt on how to legally and ethically improve their eligibility.

As an analogy, I like the example of a senior citizen (usually an elderly parent), who hires an attorney to help him qualify for Medicaid (I always get "Medicaid" mixed up with "Medicare." I'm pretty sure I mean Medicaid) in case he needs to go to a nursing home.[26]

In college financial aid planning, we don't use trusts or other legal instruments employed by Elder Law attorneys, and there's no five year "look back period," but the principles are the same – we shelter assets to improve eligibility for benefits.

Note how your eligibility may be unaffected by how much money you've saved. Because if you've stashed your money, in the "wrong" places, you might be able to reallocate your assets into "buckets" that penalize you less severely, or don't penalize you at all.

Example: Family A and Family B[27] can have substantially the same amount of income, assets, home equity, children and so forth, for example:

Adjusted Gross Income:	$150,000
Number of Children:	3
College Funds:	$200,000
House Value:	$800,000
Mortgage balance:	$400,000
Retirement Savings	$375,000

---

[26] The "Medicaid Spend down."

[27] Do you know the B's? Great family, but Mr. B has a bit of a drinking problem.

How to REALLY Pay "Wholesale" for College
Andrew Lockwood, CollegeSuccessBulletin.com

Children from each family apply to the exact same schools, but Family A will end up paying full price, possibly taking on large amounts of college debt that will haunt them and their children for years.

Family B, on the other hand, will send their children to the same colleges for a 25-30% (or more) discount, reducing or avoiding their reliance on pricy student loan debt to pay for college.

The Wall Street Journal put it best – "It's not how much money you've saved, it's where you've saved that money."

So let's see how the financial aid office calculates how much – or how little – financial aid it will award.

How to REALLY Pay "Wholesale" for College
Andrew Lockwood, CollegeSuccessBulletin.com

CHAPTER 6

EFC AND THE "DOUBLE-SECRET" FORMULA

Did you know that the U.S. government – specifically, the Department of Education – has its own particular way of calculating how much you can afford to pay for college?

And their rules are followed by almost every college in the country?

Yup. Just fill out the FAFSA, hit the "submit" button and Presto! out spits your Expected Family Contribution, otherwise known as EFC.

That number represents the amount of money that the government, in all of its wisdom and glory, thinks you can afford to pay for one year of higher education. NOT necessarily what you will pay, but what you appear to be able to afford under the formulas, known as the "Federal Methodology."

Factors include: income, number of family members in college, assets of the parent, assets of the child and more. (Don't worry, I'll explain this again. And again.)

Wondering what your EFC is? I'll tell you how to estimate it – in a minute.

WARNING – you will probably be very angry, shocked, confused or depressed by your EFC.

Why? The average EFC for a family earning $120,000 in adjusted gross income is roughly $30,000.

You read that correctly – a family earning a low six-figure income – before paying income taxes, property taxes, the mortgage and all of the other expenses associated with modern life– is expected to be able to pay $30,000 per year toward college.[28]

The biggest flaw in the EFC formula is that it doesn't factor expenses. So if you lived in an expensive area of the country, like a suburb in the Northeast, and you earned $120,000, your EFC would be identical to a family with the same financial profile living in Sheboygan, Wisconsin, where the cost of living might be 50% less.

The good news is that you can control your EFC, with planning.

I'm no psychic, but I predict that, after you calculate your EFC, you are going to be very interested in learning how to lower it.

---

[28] I don't make these rules - don't shoot the messenger!

RESOURCE

The Department of Education helps you estimate your EFC:

http://www.fafsa4caster.ed.gov

After you figure out your EFC, watch this workshop to see how you can lower it (which boosts your eligibility for financial aid):

Wholesale4College.com/online-workshop

The "Institutional Methodology"

Approximately 200 private colleges use the CSS Profile to calculate your EFC a different way, using what's called the "Institutional Methodology."[29] One of the key differences between the Federal Methodology, used by FAFSA-only colleges, and the Institutional Methodology is that the Institutional Methodology factors in the equity you appear to have in your home (the difference between the fair market value of your home and your mortgage balances), reasoning that if you have it, you'll use it by pulling a home equity line of credit (compared to a high rate, high fee parent loan or private student loan).

There are exceptions. Harvard's website is very clear that it does NOT count home equity against you, for example (with an endowment valued at more than $30 Billion, Harvard probably won't lose sleep over giving you a few extra bucks).

---

[29] This term is a bit of a misnomer, since there is no published formula pertaining to the Institutional Methodology, the way there is with the "Federal Methodology."

How to REALLY Pay "Wholesale" for College
Andrew Lockwood, CollegeSuccessBulletin.com

Duke counts only a certain portion of the apparently available equity, not every last dollar. Example: if your fair market value is $750,000, but you owe $150,000, most CSS Profile schools would penalize you on the $600,000 (750K value less 150K owed). But Duke penalizes only up to a certain amount (they cap it) based on income level.[30]

My "back of the napkin" way to calculate EFC for a private school is to use the FAFSA Forecaster link above, then add $8,000 per $100,000 (8%) of home equity.

So if your FAFSA forecaster EFC is $30,000 and you figure out you have $200,000 in home equity (fair market value of your home less all outstanding mortgages and equity lines), your EFC could be around $46,000 - $30,000 plus $16,000.

RESOURCE: Since October 2011, the Department of Education has required colleges to post a "Net Price Calculator" on their respective websites. Although potentially confusing (there's no standardized set of information they must ask), I think this is a great first step, because it helps families see that they may not have to pay "Sticker Price" for college.

Here's the link to the College Board's Net Price Calculator:

http://netpricecalculator.collegeboard.org/

Let's take a closer look at how colleges use your EFC.

---

[30] Your head hurt yet? To make things more complicated, Duke says it penalizes up to 8% of parent assets, when the Federal Methodology says 5.64%. WTF?

How to REALLY Pay "Wholesale" for College
Andrew Lockwood, CollegeSuccessBulletin.com

CHAPTER 7

THE "DOUBLE-SECRET" FORMULA IN ACTION

How to determine how much – or little – financial aid you'll get

Now, a quick (read, "oversimplified") lesson on the formula[31] used by each school to determine your financial aid award. Here it is:

COA

EFC

= NEED

COA is short for "Cost of Attendance" – one year of tuition, fees, room and board, etc.

EFC is (still) Expected Family Contribution –a formulaic number that indicates how much you can afford to pay for one year of college, according to the Department of Education. (Calculated

---

[31] Can you believe that it's taking me all these chapters to get to this point? I'm shaking my head...

35
How to REALLY Pay "Wholesale" for College
Andrew Lockwood, CollegeSuccessBulletin.com

automatically after you file the FAFSA – the Free Application for Financial Aid.)

Need. Schools award financial aid based on how much need you show. Once you identify the percentage of need that your college meets, you have a decent handle on what your award will look like by plugging that data into the formula. Here is a simplified[32] example:

$50,000 Cost of Attendance

-$25,000 EFC

=$25,000 Need

You pay your EFC plus any unmet need.

Scenario 1: 100% of Need Met

If a college meets 100% of need, you pay your EFC of $25,000 only. In other words, you cover what the formula "expects" you to cover and the college will foot the bill for the rest.

Generally, the most elite, competitive colleges in the country will meet 100% of need. I listed them at the end of this masterpiece, somewhere around page 785.[33] Most schools do not meet 100% of need, however.

---

[32] Sadly, rounded down.

[33] Hah. Had you going for a moment, mais oui? But I do list them later in this book.

Scenario 2: 90% Need Met

EFC + Unmet Need

If the college meets 90% of need, you'll pay your EFC of $25,000 PLUS the *unmet need, or $2,500*, calculated as follows: 90% of total ($25,000) need is $22,500 ($25,000 x .90).

In other words, you can expect to receive an award of $22,500, or 90% of the $25,000, meaning that you'll be responsible for the 10% ($2,500), unmet portion. You'll pay:

EFC + Unmet Need

$25K + $2,500 = $27,250

Scenario 3. 75% of Need Met

A college could meet only 75% of need, or $18,750. You can do the arithmetic on this one! ☺[34]

How can you obtain information about school generosity? Look on the websites for each college – specifically, for its Net Price Calculators. (You may have to click around for a while – every college doesn't make this info easy to find.) You can also call the financial aid office but you'll probably end up frustrated by the lack of responsiveness, according to most of the parents I work with.

Another great resource is the Common Data Set – a "clearinghouse" of data self-reported by colleges. Warning: you'll

---

[34] Cheater! You'll pay $31,250: $25,000 EFC + $6,250 Unmet Need.

How to REALLY Pay "Wholesale" for College
Andrew Lockwood, CollegeSuccessBulletin.com

see a TON of information, which can be overwhelming. Nonetheless, almost everything you'd want to know about paying for college:

Percentage of financial need met

What percentage of the average award is free (grants) versus loans and work study,

Graduation rates and

A lot (a lot!) more.

If you're the analytical, roll up your sleeves and dig in to the data type of guy/gal, the Common Data Set will be like Disney World[35] for you!

No matter whether you seek help or do it yourself, preparation and research can pay off in a big way. And blowing it off could coast tens of thousands of dollars in financial aid that was yours for the taking.

Next we'll look at some juicy loopholes that could boost your eligibility!

---

[35] Without the mandatory gift shop standing between the end of every ride and the exit.

How to REALLY Pay "Wholesale" for College
Andrew Lockwood, CollegeSuccessBulletin.com

CHAPTER 8

SOME "STUFF" COUNTS AGAINST YOU MORE THAN OTHERS...SOME NOT AT ALL!
Deciphering the twisted, counter-intuitive Financial Aid Regulations

OK, here's where it gets complicated. But it's also where the opportunities lay, so listen up!

In summary, "kid stuff" – assets and income – counts against you more than "parent stuff." Here's how.

In the formulas, parent assets are penalized between 5.64% and 12%[36]. In other words, $100,000 of parent money will gross up your EFC - reduce your eligibility – by $5,640.

If you held that same $100,000 in your child's name, your EFC would increase by 20% or 25%.[37] Your EFC penalty would be $20,000 or $25,000!

---

[36] From the "Too Geeky to Matter" Department: it's really 5.64%, having to do with how the formulas convert assets to income. And some schools – Duke is one of them – penalize 8%. Some parents say they've heard 12%. But hear me now and believe me later - just use 5.64%!

How to REALLY Pay "Wholesale" for College
Andrew Lockwood, CollegeSuccessBulletin.com

By contrast, if I took that 100G's and went to Vegas (I'm soooooo "money"), I'd be eligible for $20,000-$25,000 more financial aid per year than you, because my questionable behavior removed that asset from my financial aid balance sheet. I'm rewarded for being irresponsible!

Not to get too political,[38] but this amounts to a penalty for doing the right thing – saving money for your child!

Speaking of disincentives, student income is penalized more severely than parent income. The parent income penalty is between 22-47% on a sliding scale, and a large chunk is excluded (this is known as the "Income Protection Allowance").

On the other hand, student income gets dinged 50% from the get-go – there's no excluded amount.

A "Cray-Cray" Example

Check this out – if your kid is hard working enough to earn $10,000 and save it, he'll pay:

Income taxes on the earnings

A 50% financial aid "penalty" on the earnings

A 20% penalty on the money he stuck in his savings account (25% at some schools)

---

[37] This depends on the college. Some private colleges assess a 25% penalty, most private and all public use 20%.

[38] Don't bait me!

So he'll net $1,000-$1,500 if he's lucky! He'd be better off sitting out, not working.[39]

Bad Advice On Where To Save

Back to savings accounts and the advice that your well-intentioned CPA or "Wealth Manager" gave you to set up child savings accounts – UGMA's, UTMA's, typically. He told you to do this because of the tax benefits (lower rates, you withdraw money without penalty), but that advice will bite you in the rumpus! It could disqualify you for grants, scholarships and other financial aid because your penalty is 20% instead of the 5.64% you'd pay if you kept the funds in your own name.

Or zero if you sheltered it!

529 College Savings Accounts

Under the Federal rules, 529 accounts are parent assets, meaning they are penalized at a lower rate (they used to be considered a child asset until Congress changed things in 2006) instead of 20% for a child asset.

Any 529 owned by a parent, naming the child as the beneficiary, is a parent asset on the FAFSA.

What about 529's owned by a grandparent, naming the child as a beneficiary?

---

[39] Calling John Galt! Oops, guess I got political.

NOT an asset reported on the FAFSA! But before you call up Grandma, here are two caveats:

1. When Grandma withdraws 529 funds to pay for college, FAFSA treats that amount as INCOME to the child. In other words, it levies a stiff 50% penalty on those funds.

2. So far, this discussion pertains to FAFSA only. In my experience (and that of my colleagues in other parts of the country), many private colleges and universities that use the CSS Profile will treat the 529 as a child asset and reduce your eligibility sharply (by 20-25%).

What do you do if you have a 529?

It may pay to sell it early, but understand that you will pay a penalty if you do not use the funds for "Qualified Higher Education Expenses" (tuition, books, room and board) if attending at least half-time. The penalty is 10% of the earnings on the 529. (Good news/bad news: earnings haven't been all that great lately. The penalty may not be terrible, it depends on your "cost basis" – what you invested.)

If you received a deduction for investing in the 529 (some states give you one), you may have to "recapture" your deduction, meaning reverse it. Work through this stuff with someone competent before you start moving your 529's willy-nilly.

Trusts

Occasionally, parents ask me whether trusts are a good idea for college financial aid planning. The answer is usually no. Trusts naming kids as beneficiaries are not exempt, they count. The "corpus," or assets held by the trust, are penalized at the child rate.

Practically all trusts allow the trustee to use funds to pay for the child's education, so this treatment in the financial aid regulations makes sense. However, in the case where the trust restricts the child's access to the funds until a certain age, like 21 or 30, you may succeed in an argument to the financial aid office that the trust assets should not be considered as resources that can be used to pay for college (if that's truly how the trust documents read).

Financial aid officers have "Professional Judgment," or discretion, to consider the story beyond the proverbial four corners of the financial aid forms (more on this topic later)

Here's a summary of parent and student stuff:

	Parent	**Child**
Income	22-47% (some excluded[40])	50% (none excluded)
Assets	5.64% (some excluded[41])	20-20% (none excluded)

Next, we'll look at exempt assets – savings that don't count against you at all!

---

[40] Income Protection Allowance
[41] Asset Protection Allowance

How to REALLY Pay "Wholesale" for College
Andrew Lockwood, CollegeSuccessBulletin.com

CHAPTER 9

EXEMPT ASSETS: THE FOUR HORSEMEN

"Loopholes" that could multiply your eligibility

The legal department (OK, me – I'm on a budget and Dershowitz won't return my calls) warned me to issue this weasel-like, lawyerly disclaimer:

Nothing in this chapter or book is meant as LEGAL ADVICE. Sometimes this stuff works, sometimes it doesn't!

Neither is it FINANCIAL ADVICE. I am not a licensed stockbroker, insurance guy, etc.[42] And even if it works for financial aid purposes, it may not be suitable for financial PLANNING purposes.

In other words, advice may work in terms of improving eligibility for financial aid, but you'd better consider carefully the legal, tax and all other non-financial aid implications. Talk to a

---

[42] Although I did serve as in-house counsel to a publicly traded brokerage company in Miami, back in the 90's. I was responsible for supervising idiot brokers who ripped off widows and orphans...fun! :)

qualified professional advisor about this stuff instead of just blindly taking my advice at face value.[43]

Last, a note on lying on the forms:

Don't lie.

Seriously, do you need me to say this?

First off, everyone knows that people who lie on the FAFSA don't go to heaven.

Second, the penalties for fraud on the FAFSA include stiff fines (10 G's) and jail time. So you AND your kid could each go away next year, she'll have a normal roommate at college, yours could be named "Bubba" up at the Big House.

Schools have gotten better at detecting fraud, too. And more aggressive about requesting "Verification" on financial aid forms when a red flag (inconsistent answers, mostly) triggers heightened scrutiny.

Enough double-talk! Let's look at five classes of assets that are exempt in the financial aid formulas.

1. Retirement Accounts (401K, 403b, 457, IRA, SEP, SIMPLE, etc.)

2. Annuities

---

[43] Unless you are any of my kids or wife. In that case, just do what I want, don't question me.

How to REALLY Pay "Wholesale" for College
Andrew Lockwood, CollegeSuccessBulletin.com

3. Insurance with cash value

4. Primary residence (FAFSA schools only)

5. Business Assets[44]

Some comments on each:

Retirement Accounts.

Under the Federal rules, the value of your retirement accounts (401K, 403B, 457, IRA, SEP, SIMPLE, etc.) is not considered an "investment" and should not be included as a parent asset. They don't count against you.

But any contributions you make to your retirement account in the "Base Year" (the tax year ending before the academic year – if your student heads to college in Fall 2016, the base year is 2015) count as income!

In other words, if you lowered your Adjusted Gross Income by $15,000 because of your retirement contribution – from $165,000 down to $150,000 – FAFSA considers your income to be $165,000, and will penalize you about 47% of that increase – almost $8,000.

So the asset is exempt, but the act of contributing to the account isn't. Stupid, right?

---

[44] Yeah, I know I said "Four Horseman." Consider this a bonus (and "Five Horseman" didn't have the same ring).

How to REALLY Pay "Wholesale" for College
Andrew Lockwood, CollegeSuccessBulletin.com

I think so. If there's a public policy behind the rules along the lines of "Parents shouldn't have to rob their retirement savings to pay for college," why is the ACT of saving that money penalized?

Despite this screwy financial aid issue, you'll never hear me advise anyone to stop funding their IRA or 401K, because you can never have enough retirement savings. But do so with your eyes wide open about the implications.

Annuities

Annuities are exempt under the FAFSA, meaning that any annuities that you own will not count as "investments" under the Federal rules. But there are a couple of issues that I want to call to your attention.

A year or so ago, I was conducting a workshop in Oyster Bay, Long Island, when a guy raised his hand as I was discussing annuities.

"I have paperwork at home, I'm about to buy an annuity that another college planner sold me," he said.

(Many "college planners" are licensed financial guys – stockbrokers, insurance guys. A fraction of them are a little sneaky about this – they conduct college planning workshops, get clients to hire them, advise that they can improve their eligibility by "shifting" their cash into a financial product, then mention, "Oh, and by they way, I sell annuities! What a coincidence!")

How to REALLY Pay "Wholesale" for College
Andrew Lockwood, CollegeSuccessBulletin.com

But this was not the main problem. I asked, "What colleges are on your list?"

The guy rattled off 10-11 colleges, all but two required the CSS Profile.

The issue: annuities are NOT exempt on this form. Put another way, the only person likely to benefit from the annuity purchase was the insurance guy!

Giving him the benefit of the doubt, the broker may have known that annuities were legitimate shelters on the FAFSA, but didn't understand that they don't work for CSS Profile colleges.

Turns about my workshop attendee was prepared to invest several hundred thousand dollars, which is why his insurance guy now has my photo on a dartboard somewhere.

Insurance

Cash value life insurance products are exempt on the FAFSA and CSS Profile.[45] I've witnessed numerous families improve their eligibility by moving money into a cash value life insurance policy.

---

[45] Although a teeny-tiny handful of colleges ask whether you have insurance via their supplemental financial aid forms.

I am not a licensed financial guy,[46] but let me caution you about insurance and annuities: be certain that you understand the benefits - and potential negatives – of investing in these things.

Specifically, look at the fees and make certain you understand the restrictions and penalties associated with accessing your money ("surrender charges") BEFORE you sign.

One of my favorite sayings is "Man plans and God laughs,"[47] which I learned from a client who was born in a concentration camp in Poland.

In the context of this discussion[48], the point is that you may decide to make a move after you've evaluated all the pros and cons, but your assumptions at the time of your decision may be flawed – life has a funny way of serving up unexpected stuff.

How much would it suck to go back to your broker a year later, tell him you need to get more money than you originally anticipated, only to learn that you'll pay a $12,000 surrender charge to withdraw your funds?

I recommend that to leave yourself a lot more access ("liquidity") than you think you need, even if it hurts a smidgen in financial aid eligibility.

---

[46] There's my famous weasel-clause disclaimer again!

[47] "Der mentsh trakht un got lakht" in Yiddish, if you must know. (Yes, I had to look it up...)

[48] As opposed to an annoying, existential "meaning of life," debate. This is a financial aid book.

Your primary residence.

FAFSA specifically excludes the value of your primary residence (note – investment properties and second homes ARE assets). Occasionally, people ask me whether they should shelter cash by paying off their mortgage.

As a recovering debt-laden person, I love getting this question and the mentality of the person asking. But this may not be the best idea for two reasons.

1. Colleges requiring the CSS Profile treat the primary residence as a potential resource to pay for college (e.g. pulling out a home equity line of credit), and

2. "Man plans, God laughs." I don't like the idea of tying up money in a home, then trying to get it out by borrowing.

First, you're now paying interest on money that was interest-free in the recent past.

Second, you may not be able to get it! After the 2008 mortgage meltdown, banks froze access to equity lines, cut them, and wiped them out completely in some cases.

Mark Twain's famous (non-Yiddish) quote goes something like, "A banker is a fellow who lends you his umbrella when the sun is shining, but wants it back the minute it begins to rain."

In other words, the best time to ask for money is when you do NOT need it.

How to REALLY Pay "Wholesale" for College
Andrew Lockwood, CollegeSuccessBulletin.com

Let's say you lose your job, then go to the bank for a loan to help you pay your bills. They care about your ability to pay them back more than anything else so you're 99% certain to be denied. Even if you have NO mortgage on your home and a perfect credit score, it's tough – the lending guidelines have changed big time since 2008.

Strategic Equity Management

Here is one more strategy that is definitely NOT for most – it's a little scary. Sometimes people pull money out of their home (by taking an equity line or remortgaging) and stash it in an exempt asset. The theory[49] is that, since CSS Profile colleges will treat you as though you have this resource, you might as well be proactive about doing so on your own terms, not those of the college financial aid office, in a way that will not count against you.

Before I get to the negatives (they are significant), let me flesh out the positive.

My client, Seth (not his real name) owns a home worth 750,000 with a mortgage of 175,000. His two boys were considering colleges like Boston College, MIT, Middlebury, Fairfield, Loyola University Maryland and other private schools. All are CSS Profile schools that count home equity as an asset.

Seth is self-employed, and, thanks to his accountant, shows a low, six-figure income on paper. Between his apparent home

---

[49] Created by a mortgage broker (surprise!)

How to REALLY Pay "Wholesale" for College
Andrew Lockwood, CollegeSuccessBulletin.com

equity and other savings, Seth's total includable assets were close to $800,000.

In the financial aid formulas, that $800,000 equates to a penalty of approximately $44,500. In other words, by sheltering these assets, Seth could improve his eligibility for financial aid (mostly free money from the schools on his boys' lists) by up to $44,500.

Seth took a larger mortgage (at the time, he was able to reduce his interest rate and term significantly, so his payments increased only $200 per month – there was no issue with affording the payments) and moved a chunk of his assets into his business account as a loan (I describe this strategy in the next chapter).

So he didn't consume his home equity, he pulled it out of his home, where it was "trapped in the bricks," then placed it into another safe, liquid investment. And he could make the payments, no sweat.

Several stars had to align for this strategy to make sense:

1. Seth had to be able to afford the new payments

2. He had to avoid doing something dumb with the proceeds from the refinance (jet skis, buying another property that could lose value and tie up cash)

3. He needed reasonable certainty that at least one of his kids would end up at a private college that penalized him for having equity.

This section of made me nervous to write, but it's a valid technique, on paper. It worked out: each of the colleges his boys ended up at gave substantial awards, so Seth was able to comfortably afford to send them to their top choices.

Be careful with this strategy!

OK, one more tip about how to reduce home value: when Pearl[50] does the CSS Profiles for our clients, she compares the value of the home the client gives against a Department of Commerce methodology known as the "Federal Housing Index Multiplier."

The Multiplier asks for two bits of information: when you bought your home and the purchase price. Then it calculates a value based on national averages, which in many cases is lower because the rate of appreciation across the country is typically less than areas like Long Island, Connecticut and other suburban areas where our clients tend to live.

Many homeowners wonder whether they can use the assessed value (as given by their county tax assessor) to calculate value. In my experience, assessed value is lower than the fair market value that you could sell your home for, and financial aid offices almost always tell you not to use it.

Bottom line – value is in the eye of the beholder. This technique is not failsafe (none of 'em are, actually) but it will work

---

[50] My "little lady," who handles financial aid form preparation in the office (she does the real work).

most of the time. CSS Profile colleges usually calculate your home value by a method similar to the federal Multiplier, so it's worth a shot!

How to REALLY Pay "Wholesale" for College
Andrew Lockwood, CollegeSuccessBulletin.com

How to REALLY Pay "Wholesale" for College
Andrew Lockwood, CollegeSuccessBulletin.com

CHAPTER 10

THE ULTIMATE SMALL BUSINESS LOOPHOLE

FAFSA asks self-employed people to value their business. The directions are explicit, but often overlooked, even by the best and brightest. They're buried.

Even if you're not self-employed, I'm pretty sure you'd stipulate[51] that there are multiple ways to value a business – one way if you're selling, another if you're filing taxes – you get the point. All legal.

Maybe five years ago, I was discussing this in a workshop in Parkland, Florida. I asked whether anyone there was self-employed. A guy in a nice, pinstriped suit[52] raised his hand.

"What do you do?"

"I'm a CPA."

---

[51] I could have said "agree" but I wanted to remind you that I went to law school.
[52] Unusual for Florida!

How to REALLY Pay "Wholesale" for College
Andrew Lockwood, CollegeSuccessBulletin.com

Crap, I thought. *This guy's going to argue with me about all the tax stuff...* But, being the brave, mature professional that I am,[53] I asked him how he would value his business.

Before answering, the bean counter told me that he had, in fact, done the FAFSA the previous year, his daughter was at Barnard, and other "back story" facts he felt I the rest of the people in the room needed to know, like how great her grades were and what other schools wanted her. (We disagreed.)

"OK," I said, "don't tell me the number, but tell me HOW you arrived at the value of your business."

"Well, firms like mine are valued at 1.5 times book, we have receivables, we own our building, have a mortgage..."

He was in the middle of rendering a very CPA-like, or banker-like, answer.

"How many employees do you have?" I interrupted.

"It varies – during tax season we bring in extras because we're so busy...14 employees total," he said, straightening up in his chair, proud of his bustling enterprise.

"OK. I understand your answer, and I'm not arguing. But on the FAFSA purposes, your business is worth zero," I replied.

"What? It is NOT! I got two offers this year alone to be bought out for a great multiple!" he sputtered.

---

[53] [Insert your own comment here.]

He should have been angry, but not because some meaty, financial aid hack told him that his business was worthless.

I'm the first to agree, it's tough being in business. Sometimes it feels like the world is against you – employees who need babysitting, clients who don't pay, dumb regulations and taxes, long hours. It's critical to stay positive as a business owner.

But for financial aid purposes, you've got to think strategically. Check your ego and emotions at the door. Be negative! In the bizarre world of FAFSA rules, looking "bad" means you'll get good results.

My new friend was miffed when I told him that his oversight "lost" him $8,000-10,000 in aid from Barnard. What was the mistake?

FAFSA rules say that any family-owned business that employs fewer than 100 employees has a zero value. Are your wheels turning?[54]

I have a client, Stacy, who owns a small, minority-owned business – a marketing agency. Through an inheritance, she had a stock portfolio of about $650,000, and her daughter was getting

---

[54] I hope you're not thinking, "I'm gonna fire those three sorry-asses I've been meaning to axe for five years. But if you are, I REALLY hope you don't mention who was the source of your idea. Take it easy, "Chainsaw!"

How to REALLY Pay "Wholesale" for College
Andrew Lockwood, CollegeSuccessBulletin.com

ready to apply to a highly-ranked, Jesuit institution on the East Coast.[55]

Stacy and her husband's income was low on paper, but their portfolio alone would penalize them at least $36,000 in lost eligibility.

After conferring with her CPA, Stacy "loaned" her business the entire amount, which she accomplished without selling or buying any securities, which could have triggered gains that would flow through to her tax return, in effect, removing the assets from her personal balance sheet.

The result: hefty, $30,000-plus awards each year.

Some of you may wonder, "What about schools that take the CSS Profile?" Stacy's daughter attends one of these colleges.

The CSS Profile requires business owners to divulge additional information about their business via an extra form, the Business/Farm Supplement. This form asks for the equivalent of a P&L (Profit and Loss statement) and a Balance Sheet for the current and previous years.

The main part of the CSS Profile will ask you the value of your business and number of employees.

---

[55] Whose name I would never reveal because someone from the school might read this book (hah). Hint: but its name sounds like "Kornikova."

So if business assets get disclosed on the CSS Profile, why did this strategy work for Stacy and other business owners, like Seth, whom we met in the previous chapter?

My theory has to do with how the forms look. Actually, the psychology of how they're READ. On one hand, the FAFSA and CSS Profile are very "official" looking documents – together – almost 30 pages of typed, neat information.

The Business/Farm Supplement, on the other hand, is handwritten by the applicant's accountant, and faxed and re-faxed a few times. It's messy. Viscerally, it's the less important-looking form.

Also, financial aid officers aren't necessarily investment bankers or business valuation experts, they may not know how to read a financial statement like a business owner might.

But under the so-called "Institutional Methodology," business assets factor into the calculation of net worth. Perhaps financial aid officers at CSS Profile colleges "haircut" or minimize their impact, on purpose or by default.

Even though this strategy is far from failsafe, the positive thing about it is that, if it doesn't work, you don't have any of the annoying surrender charge issues relating to insurance products or annuities, discussed in the previous chapter.

Other of my "pet" strategies for business owners include putting their children on payroll (they're taxed at a lower rate),

How to REALLY Pay "Wholesale" for College
Andrew Lockwood, CollegeSuccessBulletin.com

implementing Tuition Benefit Plans to pay for employees of the business, establishing IRAs for their children.

A full discussion is beyond the scope of this chapter, but business owners would be well-served to consult an expert on these college funding strategies for business owners.

CHAPTER 11

SEVENTEEN COSTLY FAFSA MISTAKES TO AVOID
Like A Toothbrush in a Gas Station Bathroom

Here's a short list of the most common mistakes I see when I'm reviewing previously filed financial aid forms for prospective clients. Committing these mistakes boosts your EFC and costs you thousands – even tens of thousands – of dollars in "lost" financial aid eligibility.

1. Mixing student "stuff" up with parent "stuff." FAFSA's sections switch back and forth between child and parent info. Child assets "count" against you much more than parent assets – roughly 20% compared to 5.64%. (So if your child has $100,000 in her name your EFC will increase by $20,000. That same amount treated as a parent asset results in a boost of your EFC to only $5,640.)

2. Disclosing the value of your retirement accounts (401K, 403B, 457, IRA, SEP, SIMPLE, etc.). FAFSA directions very clearly tell you NOT to include retirement accounts.

How to REALLY Pay "Wholesale" for College
Andrew Lockwood, CollegeSuccessBulletin.com

3. Disclosing the value of life insurance and annuities. FAFSA directions tell you not to include these either.

4. Including the value of your home when you answer the question about your investments. The directions tell you to exclude the value of your primary residence. NOTE – you must include values of investment properties.

5. Not indicating that you want to be considered for work study and loans. Check this box, even if you plan not to take loans or work. You're not obligating yourself, when and if you're offered these types of aid, you can refuse the offer. Say "yes" to show the financial aid office that you need money, make your final decision to accept or not, later.

6. Waiting until you've completed your tax returns before tackling the FAFSA. Many schools have priority deadlines of February 1st, February 15th and March 1st (check with each school on your list), which is long before most "normal" people file their taxes – April 15th. Submit the FAFSA with estimated information, then update it after you solidify the numbers on your 1040's. Since grants and scholarships are often awarded on a first-come, first-served basis, you'd better not slack off – get 'em in!

7. Blowing the Priority Deadlines. Many schools award money on a first come, first-served basis. Typically, all financial aid applications received before the deadline are considered equally, whether they were filed weeks or hours before.

How to REALLY Pay "Wholesale" for College
Andrew Lockwood, CollegeSuccessBulletin.com

At the risk of beating a dead horse, make sure you check two deadlines for each college on your list: the ADMISSIONS application deadline, and the PRIORITY financial aid deadline!

8. Making careless typographical mistakes – transposing digits of a social security number, date of birth, confusing parent and child dates of birth, social security numbers and so forth. These gaffes have nothing to do with the substance of your application (income, assets, etc.), but they can cause delays in processing your FAFSA – maybe two-three weeks of lost time that can cause you to miss out on the "good" aid by the time your application gets back up in the queue.

9. Over-valuing your business if you're self-employed. A close look at the directions tells you that business assets are exempt if you employ fewer than 100 employees. Big loophole!

10. Not filing. I've seen it more than once, people slog through the form, think they're done, and log out. But it ain't over 'til it's over – the FAFSA must be "signed" electronically (via a PIN for each student and parent) and submitted. Colleges don't get it until you hit the submit button!

11. Messing up the tax information: confusing adjusted gross income, reporting taxes withheld from your paycheck (instead of total taxes paid- they're different numbers) and other related errors.

12. Using a nickname instead of a given name ("Jimmy" instead of "James." Or "Cool Poppa T" instead of "Bradley.").

FAFSA may not be able to match a nickname with the social security number.

13. In the case of a divorced family, using the info for the incorrect (less advantageous, not an ex-spouse who's always wrong) parent. FAFSA's directions indicate that you should use the parent with whom the child spent the majority – more than half – of his or her time. (Note: that this is an entirely different issue than which parent declares the child as a dependent on his/her tax returns.[56]

14. Not catching mistakes on the Student Aid Report (SAR), which the Department of Education sends you a few days after you file the FAFSA. If a number is transposed, a date of birth incorrect, etc. this is another chance to catch it. Correct it immediately!

15. Failure to be consistent with the CSS Profile and other forms. Here's a common scenario:

Sean applies Early Decision to his top choice private university. He gets his application in by November 1st, his dad submits his CSS Profile at the same time. So far, so good.

December 15th, Sean gets deferred into the regular application pool.

---

[56] In many cases, divorced parents take turns claiming the child as a dependent for the tax year. So a kid can be a dependent of the mother in Year One, and the father in Year Two. But for financial aid purposes, the mom could be the custodial parent for each of Year One and Two without it being inconsistent on your tax returns.

How to REALLY Pay "Wholesale" for College
Andrew Lockwood, CollegeSuccessBulletin.com

Mid January, Sean's dad completes and submits the FAFSA, which became available January 1. So far so good.

Except it's not. In his rush to get the FAFSA in, Sean's dad didn't compare the figures he indicated on the CSS Profile two months earlier.

Turns out that he forgot to include one of his savings accounts for Sean on the CSS Profile, but included it on the FAFSA.

March, Sean finds out that his top choice school admitted him – he's psyched!

Two weeks later the financial aid award comes. It sucks.

Sean's dad calls the financial aid office to ask which of his orifices they expect him to pull tuition out of. They explain that they found some inconsistencies on his financial aid application and send Sean, not Sean's dad – a "Verification" form that, in fact, does take a close look at some of orifices! But it sits in Sean's email in-box for nine days.

Sean's dad now scrambles at the last minute to provide the additional information, hoping that things will somehow work out.

If Sean's dad had "repositioned" his assets prior to filing (legally "shifted" his savings to improve eligibility), it could come back to haunt him in the verification process – the financial aid office can now ask all sorts of questions about previous bank statements, earnings, etc., some of which may reveal a paper trail of the old amounts.[57]

Don't give the financial aid officer any reason to doubt your numbers.

16. Not filing at all for any reason. 53% of all eligible families don't even bother to file, according to one study. Hockey great Wayne Gretzky is credited with the quote, "You miss 100% of the shots you don't take." Don't leave any money on the table, don't blow off filing just because you think you earn too much.

17. Listing some, not all of the colleges you're applying to. You send the FAFSA to each school you want to consider giving you money. Don't leave off any college you or your child is applying to!

18. Failure to follow up with the financial aid office after you file, to ensure they received everything. I know, you have a printed receipt from FAFSA indicating which schools got the form, but sometimes colleges can't find your silly old FAFSA!

Don't assume anything – follow up!

(For a detailed ["excruciatingly" detailed] walkthrough of the actual pitfalls, landmines and opportunities lurking on the FAFSA,

---

[57] Verification is not as bad as an IRS audit, but it feels pretty invasive. 30% of financial aid applications are supposedly verified, but many colleges voluntarily verify 100%. One way to avoid chances of verification - using the IRS Data Retrieval Tool to submit tax returns.

check out www.iLoveFAFSA.com –yes, that's really the name of the website!)

How to REALLY Pay "Wholesale" for College
Andrew Lockwood, CollegeSuccessBulletin.com

CHAPTER 12

How High "Sticker Price" Colleges Can Cost Less Than "Cheaper" State Schools

I'm guessing you know that college is really, really, expensive.[58] You may have seen stats that back this up (college costs have risen 1,000% in the past 30 years, compared to 700% for healthcare, 300% for inflation, yada yada yada).

But what do these percentages mean? As I write this in 2013, one year at a state university can run around $20,000-45,000 (tuition, fees, room and board, etc.), depending on whether you're attending in-state or out-of-state.[59] A private college can cost more than $60,000.[60] But frequently, the net price of a seemingly more expensive college is cheaper.

---

[58] I'm rumored to have psychic powers. Look for my late night infomercial!

[59] Which I call, "The worst of both worlds" – higher rates as a non-resident, and state colleges have very little funding to give.

[60] Sadly, there are numerous state and private schools with even higher sticker prices.

How? Many private colleges and universities use their endowments to meet 85%, 90%, 95% or more of financial need. State colleges meet roughly 50-65%.

They also engage in a practice called "Leveraging," meaning that they bribe students whom they want to come. This has nothing to do with your income or assets.

The umbrella term for this type of discounting is "Merit" aid. I find this term misleading, because when most parents hear the word "merit" or "merit scholarship" they think their kid won't qualify if he doesn't have perfect SAT scores and a 5.0 average (out of 4.0).

I think the better term is "Non Need-based," because there are plenty of B plus kids who receive $8,000, $12,000, $20,000 or more per year from private colleges.

(This weekend I ran into a client's kid, who was bussing tables at a new Italian place that opened up on the beach near our house. She had a C plus average and a heavy weed habit. But she got $22,000 per year from her top choice school!)

Colleges apply leveraging strategies to attract kids from affluent families, kids from parts of the country that are underrepresented at that college, etc. because they need to get tushies in seats![61] If they charge 60K, but give a family earning 300K a discount of 12K, two things happen:

1. They still get 48K from the family; and

---

[61] Critics point out that this practice has resulted in less funding going to low income families.

2. The kid gets to feel good that she earned a scholarship (and Mom gets to throw it in the face of her annoying sister-in-law who brags daily about her "Perfect" daughter at Penn).

Since the mid-1990s, colleges have given more merit-based aid than need-based.

The average discount rate at private colleges is 45%.[62] Average!

(To learn how colleges must use their endowments, watch this presentation: EndowmentScholarships.com)

A recent CNBC story claimed that 50% of students attending college receive a 90% discount! I guess this is mathematically possible, but it seems high even to me (but they won't respond to my emails).

Who gets this money? Not just low-income families – the majority goes to families from the top income quartile.

Which colleges do not give to six-figure-earning families? State universities. Not all, but most of are not generous to "Forgotten Middle Class" families[63].

The Cost of Attendance at state universities - paying in-state tuition rates – runs around $25,000 at most schools. If you're an out-of-stater, it's close to $50,000 in many cases, at least $40,000 across the board.

---

[62] This stat comes from a great book, *College Unbound*, by Jeff Selingo. Highly recommended.

[63] That's my term - I made it up. Nice, huh?

Colleges use "Net Price Calculators" to show stuff like the following:

How to REALLY Pay "Wholesale" for College
Andrew Lockwood, CollegeSuccessBulletin.com

	State University	Private College
Cost	$45,000	$60,000
Discount:	0	$18,000
Net Price:	$45,000	$42,000

(I work through this example in my workshops – you can watch a recorded one here: Wholesale4College.com/online-workshop,)

Other factors to consider besides yearly out of pocket costs:

Many students at large public school report:

Their classes have 300-500 students enrolled;

They're forced to watch an instructor on a television monitors; and

Their instructor is not a "real" professor, but rather a graduate assistant from a former Soviet Bloc country with a thick accent.

There's one more important factor, which I'll get to in the next chapter.

My last comment is that I am definitely NOT bashing public colleges at all, many kids can handle them. But it's important to have your eyes wide open about this stuff. And it's smart and fair to discuss what your child's learning environment could look like. It's great for some kids, not so for others.

Now, let's look at how long it takes to get out of college.

CHAPTER 13

HOW LONG DOES IT REALLY TAKE TO GRADUATE?

The Six Year Plan

It's not so easy to get out of a public college in four years. 58% of college students take six years to get their degree. SIX years!

Guess what the main culprit is? Hint: it's not because:

Kids are goofing off and cutting class;

They're smoking happy grass or partying too much; or

They're aimlessly switching majors and prolonging their college careers.

Sure, these issues contribute to the problem, but they're not the main source.

The main reason is that *students can't get classes they need to fulfill their major!*

Classes are oversubscribed, it's very hard to get a slot in a required course.

It's not just because of overcrowding. Once they get tenure, professors have an easier time managing their massive teaching load (1-2 classes per semester) – they can teach Wednesdays at 11am even if it doesn't suit most students' schedules.

Here's a common scenario: if you're a business major, you may not get Accounting 101 until your Junior year – and Accounting 102 for another two or three semesters. You're lower in priority than the 5th year, 4th year and other students who have been trying to get that class longer than you.

State universities are facing the perfect storm – budget cuts to prevent them hiring more staff and swelling enrollment. Their labor costs and costs of implementing state-of-the-art, cutting edge technology pose formidable budgetary constraints too. Every state in the Union is crying the blues about being underfunded. I don't see this environment improving in the near term, if ever. Do you?[64]

Check out these statistics reported by the Education Trust for a handful of public RWSCs Rear Window Sticker Colleges[65]):

College	Four Year Graduation Rate

---

[64] That's a rhetorical question - don't feel pressured to answer.
[65] You know, the same schools everyone from your high school applies to. I made up that term, too – can you hear me patting myself on the back?

How to REALLY Pay "Wholesale" for College
Andrew Lockwood, CollegeSuccessBulletin.com

University of Maryland	66.1%
University of Michigan	72.9%
University of Delaware	64%
Ohio State University	51.1%
SUNY Binghamton	65.9%
SUNY Oneonta	52%
Penn State	63%
University of Wisconsin (Mad.)	51.9%
UMASS Amherst	51.6%
UNC – Chapel Hill	75.2%
University of Virginia	86.8%
West Virginia University	32.5% (!)

Although these numbers are dismal, there are some bright spots (UVA, UNC). Your best bet is to plan on taking five years to graduate, but do whatever you can to stack the odds of a four-year sojourn in your favor (load up on AP classes, take a couple of summer classes, etc.) Now let's look at some private RWSCs:

How to REALLY Pay "Wholesale" for College
Andrew Lockwood, CollegeSuccessBulletin.com

Private College	Four Year Graduation Rate
Emory	82.5%
Fairfield	79.1%
Penn	87.2%
Cornell	86.7%
Boston College	86.9%
Boston University	65.1%
George Washington University	75.7%
Syracuse	69.7%
Villanova	87.5%
Lehigh	78.2%
Bucknell	87.4%
Northwestern	85.5%
Stanford	78.9%
Harvard	86.8%
MIT	85.1%
USC	73.3%
Bentley	80.3%
Babson	86.8%
High Point	52.6%
Elon	77.5%

How to REALLY Pay "Wholesale" for College
Andrew Lockwood, CollegeSuccessBulletin.com

Williams	89%
Duke	88.5%
Vanderbilt	86.5%

With exception (High Point, Boston University), you have a much better shot at completing your degree in four years at a private college, which typically has smaller classes and fewer over-enrollment issues.

How to REALLY Pay "Wholesale" for College
Andrew Lockwood, CollegeSuccessBulletin.com

How to REALLY Pay "Wholesale" for College
Andrew Lockwood, CollegeSuccessBulletin.com

CHAPTER 14

SOME COLLEGES ARE BETTER GIVERS THAN OTHERS

Although colleges use the same financial aid formulas, they differ significantly in how much they award. In other words, there are discrepancies about how they APPLY the financial aid formulas.

Generally speaking, older, prestigious colleges – Ivies and other private universities, a smattering of state schools (UVA, UNC, the University of Michigan[66]) – offer significant amounts of aid thanks to their large endowments. Public universities offer very little financial aid as they rarely have endowment funding to spare. Instead, they award federal grants and loans.

All things being equal – like school reputation, how alums fare in the job market, "fit" and so forth – wouldn't you rather attend a school with more grants and scholarships?

---

[66] Although these state universities have large endowments, they favor in-state students when they award financial aid. In my experience, it's highly unlikely for a New Yorker to get a significant award from Michigan, even if she demonstrates a decent amount of financial need.

How to REALLY Pay "Wholesale" for College
Andrew Lockwood, CollegeSuccessBulletin.com

Ask (research) these three questions:

1. What percentage of financial need does the college meet?

2. How is that need met (the percentage of free stuff vs. loans and work study)?

3. What happens in years two, three, etc.? If your financial need stays the same, will your financial aid AWARD look substantially the same?

I created a webinar that walks you through exactly how to research generosity (and more), using the tools offered by the College Board, Net Price Calculators (described above) and the Common Data Set: www.Wholesale4College.com/research-class.

You can also consult the rankings magazines – US News and World Report, Princeton Review, Kaplan, etc.

Don't assume that similarly-ranked colleges are equally generous.

How to REALLY Pay "Wholesale" for College
Andrew Lockwood, CollegeSuccessBulletin.com

CHAPTER 15

"FORGOTTEN MIDDLE CLASS" FAMILIES RECEIVE JUICY GRANTS AND SCHOLARSHIPS

For more than a decade, colleges and universities have publicly courted upper middle class families – regularly awarding five figure sums to parents with six figure incomes. Another reason you should not blow off filling out the financial aid paperwork, even if you think you won't qualify. One study showed that 53% of eligible families did not bother applying – leaving millions on the table.

Look at this information from the University of Pennsylvania – note how many high-income earners receive need-based financial aid for their incoming freshman in 2013:[67]

---

[67] http://www.sfs.upenn.edu/paying/paying-pro-look-at-the-facts.htm

Income	Median Total Awards	% Applicants Offered Aid
0-39K	60,505	100
40K-69,999	56,425	99
70K-99,999	50,500	96
100K-129K	41,040	99
130K-159K	35,700	97
160K-189,999	28,150	81
190K-219,999	19,530	76
220,000-up	16,870	28

Plenty of six-figure-earning families receive substantial awards at Penn – and many private colleges, for that matter.

Wondering what Penn's aid packages look like – are they loans or grants? Almost 100% of Penn's financial aid award packages consist of free stuff – grants. (Penn, like all Ivies and other competitive schools, does not give merit money. No scholarships for grades, athletic ability, musical talent, etc.) [68]

---

[68] Note - I had to go to the College Board website to figure this out, it wasn't on Penn's website. I show you how to do this in this webinar that I keep mentioning without any hint of shame: http://wholesale4college.com/research-class.

Here's a look at some RWSC[69] schools and the percentage of financial need they meet:

College	% Need Met
Babson	96
Bentley	96
Boston College	100
Boston University	92
U. Delaware	75
Duke	100
Elon	62
Emory	94
Fairfield	88
GW	90
Loyola (MD)	100
Lehigh	94
Northeastern	89
Northwestern	100
Penn State	59
Scranton	66
Stanford	100
Syracuse	96

---

[69] Rear Window Sticker Colleges - i.e. schools represented on the rear windows of cars in your neighborhood, defined again here in case you skipped to this page, and because I'm still proud that I came up with it.

How to REALLY Pay "Wholesale" for College
Andrew Lockwood, CollegeSuccessBulletin.com

SUNY Binghamton	66
University of Rhode Island	64
UMASS	80
USC	100
Vanderbilt	100
Villanova	82
Wake Forest	100

Source: College Board (except for Northwestern, for which I looked stuff up via the Common Data Set because there was no data on the College Board site.)

So, let's say that you're considering Villanova and Wake Forest, two similarly-ranked schools. Wake is much more generous and therefore more likely to be cheaper to attend.

All of this information is publicly disclosed, you just have to roll up your sleeves and dig it up.

CHAPTER 16

COLLEGES WITH LOOSE PURSE STRINGS

Schools that meet 100% of Financial Need

Here's a list of the most generous colleges in America, according to *US News and World Report.* No way you've heard of all of 'em!

Amherst College
Amridge University (Who?)
Barnard College
Bates College
Boston College
Bowdoin College
Brown University
Bryn Athyn College[70]
Bryn Mawr College
CalTech
Carroll University
Carleton College
Claremont McKenna
Colby College
Colgate University

---

[70] Hey, there's more than one "Bryn" college, and this one has TWO awkwardly placed Y's in its name.

College of the Holy Cross
Columbia University
Concordia University
Cornell University
Dartmouth College
Davidson College
Duke University
Emory University
Franklin W. Olin College of Engineering
Georgetown University
Gettysburg College
Grinnell College
Hamilton College
Harvard University
Harvey Mudd College
Haverford College
Macalester College
MIT
Middlebury College
Mount Holyoke College
Northwestern University
Oberlin College
Occidental College
Pitzer College
Pomona College
Princeton University
Rice University
Scripps College
Smith College
St. Olaf College
Stanford University
Swarthmore College
Thomas Aquinas College
Trinity College
Tufts University
University of Chicago

How to REALLY Pay "Wholesale" for College
Andrew Lockwood, CollegeSuccessBulletin.com

UNC –Chapel Hill
University of Notre Dame
U Penn
University of Richmond
University of Virginia
Vanderbilt University
Vassar College
Washington University-St. Louis
Wellesley College
Wesleyan University
Williams College
Yale University

This list changed slightly from my first edition, some schools dropped off (Lafayette, Reed) some found their way on (Amridge, Bryn Athyn).

How to REALLY Pay "Wholesale" for College
Andrew Lockwood, CollegeSuccessBulletin.com

CHAPTER 17

LARGEST COLLEGE ENDOWMENTS 2005 VS. 2011

StatisticBrain.com reports the following list of colleges by size of endowment (in billions)[71]:

College	Endowment 2005	Endowment 2011
Harvard University	$25,473	$31,728
Yale University	$15,224	$19,374
University of Texas	$11,610	$17,149
Princeton University	$11,207	$17,110
Stanford University	$12,205	$16,503
MIT	$6,712	$9,713
U Michigan	$4,931	$7,835
Columbia University	$5,191	$7,790
Northwestern	$4,215	$7,183
Texas A&M	$4,964	$7,000

---

[71] You weren't going to think "dollars," right?

How to REALLY Pay "Wholesale" for College
Andrew Lockwood, CollegeSuccessBulletin.com

Penn	$4,370	$6,582
U of Chicago	$4,137	$6,575
Notre Dame	$3,650	$6,260
Duke University	$3,826	$5,747
Emory University	$4,376	$5,400
Wash. U St. Louis	$4,268	$5,280
Cornell University	$3,777	$5,059
University of Virginia	$3,219	$4,761
Rice University	$3,611	$4,451
USC	$2,746	$3,517
Vanderbilt University	$2,628	$3,415
Dartmouth College	$2,714	$3,413
New York University	$1,548	$2,827
Johns Hopkins	$2,177	$2,598
U Pittsburgh	$1,530	$2,527
U Minnesota	$1,969	$2,503
Brown University	$1,844	$2,497
UNC Chapel Hill	$1,486	$2,261
U Washington	$1,490	$2,154
Ohio State University	$1,726	$2,121
Purdue University	$1,341	$2,002
U Richmond	$1,208	$1,877
U Wisconsin–Madison	$1,125	$1,873

How to REALLY Pay "Wholesale" for College
Andrew Lockwood, CollegeSuccessBulletin.com

Williams College	$1,348	$1,784
Caltech	$1,418	$1,772
Rockefeller University	$1,557	$1,746
Boston College	$1,270	$1,726
Penn. State	$1,175	$1,725
Case Western	$1,516	$1,703
Pomona College	$1,299	$1,700
Amherst College	$1,155	$1,642
University of Rochester	$1,370	$1,623
Georgia Tech	$937	$1,620
University of Illinois	$1,148	$1,601
Indiana University	$1,107	$1,575
Swarthmore College	$1,164	$1,508
Grinnell College	$1,391	$1,500
Wellesley College	$1,276	$1,500
UCLA	$668	$1,486
Smith College	$1,036	$1,430
Tufts University	$845	$1,404
Michigan State University	$906	$1,400
George Washington U	$823	$1,331
University of Florida	$836	$1,295
University of Kansas	$955	$1,250
University of Nebraska	$1,042	$1,242

Washington and Lee	NA	$1,218
University of Oklahoma	$777	$1,212
Southern Methodist U	$1,014	$1,197
Texas Christian University	$942	$1,192
Georgetown University	$741	$1,160
Boston University	$777	$1,160
Yeshiva University	$1,149	$1,125
University of Missouri	$849	$1,119
Lehigh University	$845	$1,077
Wake Forest University	$907	$1,058
U California, Berkeley	NA	$1,055
University of Iowa	NA	$1,044
Carnegie Mellon University	$837	$1,017
Tulane University	$780	$1,015
University of Cincinnati	$1,032	$1,004
Baylor University	$746	$1,004

Interestingly, the colleges with the highest endowments are NOT necessarily the most generous. NYU sucks financial aid-wise, for example. And who would have thought that the U of Minnesota would have such a war chest for the love of Kevin McHale!

Source: http://www.statisticbrain.com/college-endowment-rankings/

CHAPTER 18

THE HIDDEN TRUTH ABOUT SCHOLARSHIPS

Scholarships are fun to talk about (OK, brag!) over coffee, the water cooler or Facebook, but the ironic thing is that most financial aid comes directly from the college endowments themselves.

Personally, one of my favorite topics is weird scholarships, but I'm full of random facts.[72]

A few comments about scholarships.

You should never have to pay a service that "finds" scholarships for you. Stay far away from any company that guarantees or pressures you to sign up. I'm NOT saying that each of them is a scam, but I have yet to come across a paid service that does something that you cannot do quickly and easily yourself – at no cost.

---

[72]But if you're cut from the same cloth, check out my favorite blog post, Yesterday, a midget hired me.

How to REALLY Pay "Wholesale" for College
Andrew Lockwood, CollegeSuccessBulletin.com

There are plenty of free scholarship search sites online. Here are a few – I cannot vouch personally for any but these sites were active when I wrote this.

www.FastWeb.com

www.CollegeBoard.org

www.MeritAid.com

www.CollegeAnswer.com

www.Scholarships.com

www.CollegeNet.com

www.College-Scholarships.com

www.FastAid.com

I deal with scams in the next chapter.

First, a word on itty-bitty little scholarships. A $500 scholarship may seem like small potatoes, but most of them are renewable. So a $500 scholarship really represents $2,000, in most cases. Get a bunch of them and they start to add up.

The other thing about little scholarships is that they tend to be less competitive, because fewer kids do the work to uncover them because of the leg work involved (not YOUR kids, of course).

The above-mentioned websites, on the other hand, are pretty highly visible online and attract a lot of traffic, making your competition tougher.

There are tons of local scholarships worth checking out. The best place to start your research is your high school guidance counselor. He or she should have a list of local organizations, such as:

The Rotary Club

The Chamber of Commerce

The Elks

The VFW

Kiwanis

The Jaycees

Booster Clubs

Etc. etc. etc.

Another place to look for local scholarships is in the local paper(s). They report scholarship winners all the time. Research the entity or institution that awarded the scholarship, contact them and inquire about their scholarship qualification process. (The more work involved, the less likely your fellow competitor-peers will do the same thing.)

Also, keep in mind that there are plenty of scholarships reserved for "regular" students –kids who are not valedictorians, did not achieve perfect SAT scores and did not broker a meaningful, long-lasting peace in the Middle East during last summer's life changing 10-day trip.

How to REALLY Pay "Wholesale" for College
Andrew Lockwood, CollegeSuccessBulletin.com

Scholarships and Need-based Aid

Now let me warn you about scholarships' relationship with need-based financial aid. It is entirely possible, that after the dozens of man-hours spent researching scholarship requirements, drafting and redrafting of essays and other agony, your child will earn $2,500 in free money.

Now, fast-forward to March of the senior year of high school, as the financial aid award letters start rolling in. Each school offering you money will also ask if you received any "outside" scholarships or financial assistance.

You'll tell them "Yes, 2,500 clams from the Knights of The Holy Grail Virtual Jousting Club."

Guess what happens? The college financial aid office will reduce their award by $2,500! All of that hard work for nothing! (A "nice" financial aid office will reduce the loan portion of the award first.)

If you're not going to qualify for need-based financial aid, ignore what I just told you, it doesn't apply to merit scholarships offered by the college.

But there is big money in the federal need-based system (more than $185 Billion). If you are going to request need-based financial aid, please be careful about the amount of time you spend chasing this "loose change!"

How to REALLY Pay "Wholesale" for College
Andrew Lockwood, CollegeSuccessBulletin.com

CHAPTER 19

AVOID SCHOLARSHIP SEARCH SCAMS!

Here are a few guidelines on sniffing out a scholarship scam. Avoid "information" or other solicitations like:

> We'll guarantee you a scholarship or your money back!

> Congratulations, you're a finalist! (Even though you didn't enter any contests.)

> You cannot get this information anywhere else!

> This scholarship costs some money.

> We need your credit card number to "reserve" or "hold" this scholarship.

> Obama Wants Single Moms to Go Back to School! (A marketing gimmick for adult education providers who pay for 'leads' generated by these types of ads)

> The bottom line is that you should avoid any high-pressure

tactics or sales-pitchy language – even if you just can't seem to put your finger on why you're getting the heebie-jeebies.

If you do get scammed you should report it to some or all of the below:

How to REALLY Pay "Wholesale" for College
Andrew Lockwood, CollegeSuccessBulletin.com

Local police precinct – economic crimes

The post office (if you received direct mail and signed up with a scammy service): usps.com

Your District Attorney's Office

The Federal Trade Commission FTC.gov/scholarshipscams

The National Consumer's League Fraud Information Center – www.fraud.org

I can't speak to how fast any of these organizations will move if you report something to them, but I can say unequivocally that these entities take scholarship scams very seriously.

How to REALLY Pay "Wholesale" for College
Andrew Lockwood, CollegeSuccessBulletin.com

CHAPTER 20

THOSE COLLEGE BOARD SNEAKY SONS OF BITCHES

Pardon my salty language, but I was watching *Frost – Nixon* when I wrote this, and that phrase featured prominently in Richard Nixon's vernacular.

I've mentioned the College Board repeatedly throughout this book because they do a great job at giving important information about colleges.

They also administer the SAT, which you probably know. But let me 'learn ya a few other, interesting facts about this "Nonprofit Institution of Higher Education."

The College Board was a **student lender** until October 2007, when it was accused of…wait for it… "Deceptive marketing practices" by two attorneys general, Cuomo (NY) and Blumenthal

(CT). They settled this lawsuit, paid a stiff fine and stopped lending.[73]

The allegation? According to Connecticut Attorney General Richard Blumenthal, "The College Board provided discounted equipment and services to the schools in exchange for a coveted spot on the schools' preferred-lender lists" without disclosing this arrangement to parents or any other interested party.

Attorney General Andrew Cuomo called this arrangement "deceitful."

I'd call it a "kickback."

But that's old news. The College Board is in another line of business that you may know about, without actually knowing: selling data.

If your child has registered for the SAT, you're experiencing it first-hand: a trickle, then a flood, of direct mail from a ton of schools you never heard of.

How do these colleges find you? You guessed it, through the College Board.

For a very reasonable set up fee of $15,000 plus a not-so-reasonable 70 cents per record, colleges can search the College Board's records by:

---

[73]

http://www.bloomberg.com/apps/news?pid=newsarchive&sid=acYVwF0t1ykE&refer=us

Grades

Scores

Ethnicity

Sex

Zip Code

Other "Selects"

How big is this business? I'm not sure, but I know that Northeastern University sent 200,000 pieces of direct mail in 2012-2013. At 70 cents per head (not including the setup fee), that's a cool $140,000 the College Board made off one college alone.

There are close to 2,600 four-year colleges in the country. If 20% (only 130) of them spend half as much as Northeastern, that's a hefty $9,000,000 for the good old College Board. I have no idea if my numbers are even close, but they seem really low – they could be triple that amount, for all I know. What do you think?

No matter how you slice it, the College Board makes millions outside of its "core" test prep business.

Incidentally, the College Board has recently lost a lot of ground to its arch-rival, the ACT. So it's changing to stay competitive. Learn about the changes to the SAT:

http://collegeplanningguru.com/sat-act/

CHAPTER 21

MERIT MONEY FOR THE AFFLUENT

Let's assume that you can't qualify for need-based financial aid. It's far from Game Over.

Countless private – and many state – colleges will regularly "bribe" students of affluent families to attend their schools.

They use a nicer term for it – "Leveraging."

Why would a college do this? Here are the main reasons.

1. To raise their rankings. A student with a high grades and standardized scores will boost their US News and World Report position, so it could be worth a $15,000 tuition discount to help climb the rankings ladder. Tulane University is notorious for this.

2. To curry favor (called "Development"). Once Parker Whitebread Pewterschmidt III enrolls at a college he's lucky to get into, the college cold-callers will descend on him like a Jersey Shore cast-member hitting the tanning salon: early, often and unctuously. Their hope is that Parker will be inclined to become a loyal financial

How to REALLY Pay "Wholesale" for College
Andrew Lockwood, CollegeSuccessBulletin.com

supporter for years as he recalls his glory days over a few brewskies at Alumni Weekend (before vomiting).

3. To compete with the Ivies and other "Tier One" colleges. Ivies, "Little Ivies" like Amherst and Williams and other DIII schools in the NESCAC[74] and other conferences don't award athletic and hardly ever award merit scholarships because they don't need to. And less-competitive[75] colleges will discount the heck out of themselves to woo Ivy-caliber students away from the top schools.

4. The overriding, most important reason: to get butts in seats! Kids and parents hardly ever think about this, because they're so busy chasing colleges around, but colleges want them just as badly.

That's why many less than stellar kids get substantial merit-based awards. Three months ago, I personally witnessed two C plus/B minus clients receive awards between $15,000-22,000 per year from their top choice schools. In my experience, if a kid has at least a B plus average, there are scores of suitable colleges that would happily award similar amounts, even greater ones.

A recent Wall Street Journal article ("Student Drought Hits Smaller Universities") illustrated what could happen when colleges don't leverage – Loyola University in New Orleans is in serious trouble because of substantial under-enrollment. Their president

---

[74] New England Small College Athletic Conference. (Told you I'd work it in somehow.)

[75] NOT "lower quality" - see *Colleges That Change Lives* by the late, great Loren Pope for superb colleges that aren't considered "elite." Also www.CTCL.org.

How to REALLY Pay "Wholesale" for College
Andrew Lockwood, CollegeSuccessBulletin.com

cited Loyola's decision to cut back on leveraging merit awards as one of the main reasons for its problems.

The College Board and the Common Data set (discussed earlier) is a great source of information in this area. Look up each college's reported 'Non-Need Based Aid" average award amount.

One of my pet strategies is to have clients apply to one or two colleges solely because they compete with other schools on the applicant's list. In other words, schools that have historically vied for the same type of student.

Then, after we (hopefully) get a nice scholarship award from the strategically chosen college, we then play the offers and schools off against each other, attempting to improve them.

I cover this technique more in a below chapter on negotiations.

How to REALLY Pay "Wholesale" for College
Andrew Lockwood, CollegeSuccessBulletin.com

CHAPTER 22

DO GRADES HAVE ANYTHING TO DO WITH FINANCIAL AID AWARDS?

I wanted to address one of the biggest misconceptions about need-based financial aid – the apparent link between academic achievement and financial aid awards.

Many parents assume that their child must have outstanding grades to qualify for grants and scholarships. This is wrong.

Need-based awards are based on your Expected Family Contribution, which is used to calculate your financial need. EFC considers more than 70 factors, none of which is related to academic stuff. (It's income, assets, age of parent, number of kids in college and more.)

Broadly speaking – if you're bright enough to get in, you're in. If you need money, you get money.

Of course, there are exceptions to this rule. And I will freely confess that, all things being equal on paper between two families – identical income, assets, etc. – the child with superior academic

How to REALLY Pay "Wholesale" for College
Andrew Lockwood, CollegeSuccessBulletin.com

achievement might do better across the board than a competitor child from the other family who is not as outstanding. Even from the so-called "need-blind" colleges.

How do I reconcile this?

Financial aid officers, particularly those at elite, competitive colleges with their own institutional money, can use "professional discretion" to sweeten the offer for superior applicants once in awhile. They call it "preferential packaging."

A common example: an athlete in the Ivy League. Ivy League schools do not award athletic scholarships (contrary to what you heard from the girl at your book club who was bragging how her son got a "full ride" for lacrosse to Princeton). But athletes frequently receive more of a "grant-in-need" than their non-athletic counterparts who look nearly identical on paper, income and asset-wise. "Need" is in the eye of the beholder!

On one hand, it may seem unfair. On the other, we're talking about the college's endowment, meaning it's their money and they can do what they want with it. Frequently, endowment gifts come with certain stipulations. It's not uncommon for donors to want their bequests earmarked for athletes, musicians, kids who are going to study environmental science, help battered women, that kid of thing.

That's just the way it is, bubba! Even if you think it's unfair.

How to REALLY Pay "Wholesale" for College
Andrew Lockwood, CollegeSuccessBulletin.com

CHAPTER 23

TO ASK OR NOT TO ASK

If you check the "Yes – I want Financial Aid" box, will it hurt your chances of admission?

Lori, a slender, dark haired 40-something mom sat across from me, with a conflicted, pained expression.

"Should we apply for financial aid, or will it hurt Carly's chances of getting in?"

Carly's first choice college was Duke. She was a great student at one of the top high schools near my office, and had kick-ass extra-curricular activities.

But there was a whole other – emotional – part of her story.

Three years ago, Carly's dad, an outgoing, hard-charging, entrepreneurial guy, died in a freak accident.

Lori felt that her husband would have wanted Carly to go to the best school she could, no matter what the price, as a reward for her hard work. After all, he left Lori with a sizeable life insurance payout (although, after Lori paid off the mortgage and took a look at college costs for her two kids, it didn't seem as much).

Here's the first part of what I told her.

Need Blind

Duke is "need-blind" – meaning they make admissions decisions without regard to whether the applicant needs financial aid. That's the party line at Duke and every need-blind school, at least.

Is this really true? First, no admissions or financial aid officer at any need-blind college will admit, on the record, that they consider whether a child wants financial aid.

They say that, if your child is good enough to get into a college, whether he or she needs financial aid is a separate issue. That's why financial aid offices and admissions offices are frequently located in separate wings, even separate buildings – to keep things apart.

Most need-blind colleges are highly competitive – they admit less than 20% - sometimes less than 10%, even 6% - of their applicants. They reject thousands of applicants for every one they admit.

Need Aware

The other category is "Need Aware" colleges – those that consider whether the applicant wants financial aid as ONE of the many factors evaluated (grades, strength of course load, standardized test scores, recommendations, etc.) They lump kids into two categories.

When an application comes in, it gets placed in one of two piles – those who requested aid ("Needs Aid") or those who didn't request aid ("Full Pricers"). Each pile is huge.

A college knows ahead of time that 70% of its freshman class will receive aid and 30% will not. (I'm making up these numbers, but they are fair.) If the admissions officer from an elite college rejects one candidate from the "Needs Aid" pile, there are still thousands of wannabes to take up the slack.

Same with the Full Pricers.

So that's the textbook explanation of the two types of colleges. Let's look at reality.

I told Lori, "Look, I can't imagine what you guys went through, but I think I understand. Even though Duke says it's Need Blind, I still feel like if you apply for financial aid, it could hurt your chances of getting in by a scintilla of a hair of a percentage point.

"It's embarrassing, but I guess I'm saying that I have no rational basis for my feelings – I'm just superstitious! If it were my daughter, I wouldn't check the box."

How to REALLY Pay "Wholesale" for College
Andrew Lockwood, CollegeSuccessBulletin.com

"OK," she said. "What if somehow Carly manages to get in, and then we back and fill out the financial aid forms?"

Again, I gave another one of my boilerplate answers.

"I can almost promise you that you will lose out – probably not entirely, but you will receive 10%, 20% or some amount less than if you had applied for financial aid at the outset.

Why? Because admissions officers and financial aid officers know EXACTLY what you're doing. They're not idiots. Really – in many cases they're a whole lot more shrewd than you'd believe – they've seen it all.

"I think you'll get less because they don't like the way you've played the game. They'll still award some money – in many cases a decent amount – but probably not as much as you could have gotten had you been honest with them in the beginning.

"They don't want to feel that you've tried to 'game" the system, especially because you'll be re-applying for financial aid each year, so this is the start of a four-year relationship.

"Are you willing to take that risk," I asked

"Yes, I really feel that it's what Jeff would have wanted," Lori replied.

"I get it. OK, that's what we'll do."

Carly applied Early Decision. Duke deferred to the main, regular decision pool, which Lori and I joked was a major

How to REALLY Pay "Wholesale" for College
Andrew Lockwood, CollegeSuccessBulletin.com

accomplishment, since Carly was a "Plain White Girl" from Long Island.[76]

Carly submitted applications to several other schools. As she started to get acceptances, we quickly submitted the financial aid applications.

Then, one day in early March, Lori called me.

"Carly got into Duke!"

"Whoa – that's awesome!" I said. "Let's get the financial aid forms in ASAP!"

"What should we say about why we didn't apply before?" She asked. "And can they cancel her acceptance?"

"Let's just tell them that Carly's guidance counselor said that she wouldn't qualify (true), so she didn't bother applying, " I said. "No way would Duke rescind their offer, either."

We rushed in the financial aid applications. A week or so later, we hear back – loans only, for $5,500. Crap.

"Is this because we delayed filing?" Lori asked (the original deadline was November 1st, it was now the middle of March).

---

[76] Competitive schools like Duke reserve up to 80% (not a misprint) of their slots for non-academic reasons: recruited athletes, legacies, minorities, international students and other "hooks." See *Admissions Confidential* by Rachel Toor.

How to REALLY Pay "Wholesale" for College
Andrew Lockwood, CollegeSuccessBulletin.com

"I'm sure that has something to do with it, but we should definitely appeal this award. It's not like Duke ran out of money in the last couple of months," I said.

So we put together a letter, outlining information that Duke didn't know, including that Lori had just returned to the workforce part-time, and her assets were really life insurance proceeds that constituted the bulk of her savings – she had little in the way of IRAs or other retirement savings, and had eight years of college expenses ahead.

The financial aid officer assigned to Lori was responsive and really nice, writing a long, heartfelt reply along the lines of "Let me see what I can do."

Two weeks later, the revised offer arrived: $17,000 in grants!

Lori was thrilled, I was ecstatic. And I imagined that Jeff was looking down, also happy.

CHAPTER 24

THE PROS (NOT CONS) OF APPLYING EARLY

Why do kids apply Early Decision? First, a note on the difference between ED (what we in the biz call it) and Early Action. If you apply ED and if are accepted, you must attend.[77] There is a "financial out" if you can't afford to come after you evaluate your financial aid package)?

Early Action is non-binding.

ED boosts chances of admission. EA barely helps, if at all.

A few stats

---

[77] Even though people younger than 18 are "minors" and lack the legal capacity to enter into a contract, ED is just that – an offer (from the kid –"If you admit me, I'm coming!") and an acceptance ("OK!" from the college.)

How to REALLY Pay "Wholesale" for College
Andrew Lockwood, CollegeSuccessBulletin.com

College	Early Acceptance Rate	Overall Rate
Harvard	18.43	5.8
Princeton	18.29	7.3
Stanford	11.88	5.7
Yale	14.26	6.7

I pulled these from a couple of sources, the *New York Times* and *Bloomberg*. You can do your own research and learn the same thing – applying early multiplies your chances of admission.

NYT article: http://www.nytimes.com/interactive/2012/12/20/education/choice-early-admission-chart-2013.html

Bloomberg article: http://www.bloomberg.com/news/2013-03-28/princeton-offers-admission-to-7-3-of-applicants-for-2013-2014.html

On the other hand, stronger students tend to apply early, so the pool of applicants is self-selecting, which you should also consider.

Next, let's look at the potential negative effect applying ED could have on your financial aid package!

How to REALLY Pay "Wholesale" for College
Andrew Lockwood, CollegeSuccessBulletin.com

CHAPTER 25

WILL APPLYING EARLY HURT YOUR CHANCES OF FINANCIAL AID?

Even the Early Bird gets screwed sometimes

You know that applying Early Decision and Early Action dramatically help your chances of admission. But what's the effect on financial aid awards?

My feeling, admittedly based on anecdotal evidence[78]– is that you'd better be careful about applying Early Decision if you need financial aid.

Why? Sometimes colleges will intentionally under-award an applicant who deserves more on paper. Guess why this happens?

Because colleges would rather that you pay more instead of less! Genius, isn't it?[79]

---

[78] As opposed to the rigorous scientific data elsewhere in this treatise!
[79] Now you see why I get the big bucks.

So it's as if the financial aid officer is sitting there with your file, thinking "Hmmm, Brandon deserves $27,000...but let's see if he'll come for $18,500? Bwah hahahahaha!!!"

That's a slight exaggeration of what goes on...I think. But the concept is important:

If you are contractually bound to attend a college, you lose a big bargaining chip in terms of financial aid.

Last year, my client Claire ignored my advice[80] and applied ED to Emory.

On December 15th, she received great good news – she got in!

The bad news came two days later – her parents got shafted in financial aid – a bunch of loans, no free money.

"What happened," her dad Scott asked. "Was it because we applied Early Decision?"

"I'm sure that had something to do with it, but this is awful," I said. "I think it's one of two things," I said. "Either they made some kind of mistake, which I doubt, or they think you make more money than you show on paper," I said.(Ironically, a few weeks later, the *New York Times* wrote a story about exactly this practice, featuring Emory! http://www.nytimes.com/2012/12/23/education/poor-students-struggle-as-class-plays-a-greater-role-in-success.html?pagewanted=all&_r=1&

---

[80] Gratifying!

Scott is a self-employed professional, who lives in an affluent area but does not show a lot of income on his tax returns.

So we were faced with a strange task – showing somehow that Scott DIDN'T make more money. Proving a negative! (Weird, right?)

When Scott called Emory's financial aid office, they asked him a few questions, one of which was about his mortgage payments. They couldn't see how Scott could afford them.

"Actually, we just finished refinancing to lower our payment," Scott told the financial aid officer.

"OK, send us the new mortgage statement and proof that you paid it,' was Emory's response.

But there was a little hitch – Claire had to either accept Emory's offer or withdraw her application by January 15th.

"Will you reassess our financial aid award by then?" Scott asked.

"We'll get back to you by April." (!)

Scott called me with this update. "How can we possibly make a decision if we don't know what our award will be?" he asked.

"That's outrageous!" I said. "But I don't have an answer. In the formulas, you deserve at least $20,000. I seriously doubt that they'll give you all of that at this point," I said, brimming with optimism.

"They could give you nothing, they could give you 10 grand. You either have to roll the dice or withdraw your application, I don't see any other options."

They decided to gamble and accept. Days later, the *New York Times* article came out, we emailed it to each other simultaneously.

"Is this what you were talking about?" Scott wrote.

"Yes!" I replied.

It had to have helped on some level – Emory increased its award to $38,000! (www.Wholesale4College.com/testimonials)

Collectively, we breathed a massive sigh of relief. This was a minor miracle, in my opinion. Appeals that start from "zero" rarely work out THIS well. But I hope you see that it's always worth going to the mat with a financial aid office, even after they give you a crappy award. It's just easier when you have other offers on the table.

Be very careful about applying ED!

CHAPTER 26

"BLACK HAT" NEGOTIATING TACTICS

How to improve a crappy financial aid offer...even if you don't have compromising photos of the Dean

Before we get to the nuts and bolts of this chapter, did you know that your financial aid award is an offer? Many parents do not understand this – they assume that the award letter is final – a "take it or leave it" proposition. It's not.

Let me share a concept that could pay off in a big way.

You can appeal a financial aid award. And if you're comparing offers from competing, similar schools – like George Washington and Syracuse, for example – NOT Princeton vs. Big Lou's Air Conditioning Lyceum[81] – you can play them off against one another, sometimes even when a colleges says "We don't do that here." Here are my suggestions on how to do this.

1. Your tone should be courteous, grateful and respectful – not pissy, angry or entitled. (I had a client who told his son's first

---

[81] They recruited me for basketball.

choice school, "Please tell me how you can justify charging $15,000 more per year than Tulane..." That appeal did not go far.) You get more flies with honey than vinegar[82].   Start the letter by thanking the financial aid office for its generous offer.

2. CC the letter to the person in admissions assigned to your file. Most admissions offices divide up the country by region, assigning officers to areas of the country.

3. Understand that the admissions department cares very much about "Yield" – the number of applicants compared to the number of students who actually matriculate on campus. The higher the yield, the better the college looks in US News and World Report, among its college peers and in the eyes of God, quite frankly.

4. Explain that, while the offer on the table is generous, the other, competitor college's offer is better.

5. Explain that your child would MUCH prefer to attend your fine institution, but without additional aid, this dream will, alas, go unfulfilled.

6. If your child is exceptional in any meaningful way (yes, I realize your child is special – and above average – but that's not what I mean) – this is your opportunity to highlight that and "resell" the college on why your student will add to the college community.

---

[82] Assuming you actually want flies. (I never really understood this expression...)

How to REALLY Pay "Wholesale" for College
Andrew Lockwood, CollegeSuccessBulletin.com

Admissions officers at competitive colleges try to "build classes," meaning they look closely at what each child potentially brings to the table and what he'll bring to the college community. They'll look for athletes, drama students, journalists, musicians, politically active students and so forth.

A great book that gives vivid, easily understood and gripping insight into this process is *The Gatekeepers* by Jacques Steinberg, former Education Writer for the New York Times. It's a behind-the-scenes look at the admissions process at Wesleyan University (full disclosure – that's my alma mater.)

Another resource to walk you through all of the possible arguments to make: my webinar, www.AppealsClass.com.

7. Another tip – without going overboard, do not hesitate to tell the financial aid office about certain hardships that may not have been disclosed within the "four corners" of the financial aid application you submitted. This is your chance to let it all hang out – do not let your pride or shame get in the way – be emotional and be very, very descriptive if you are comfortable doing so.

Check that – do this even if you're not so comfortable! The stakes are too high to let your ego get in the way.

8. My final word of advice on this topic is do NOT, ahem, "bluff!" Don't get cute and imply that you received a better award elsewhere unless it's completely true. Because the financial aid office you're writing to will probably want to see a competing offer.

How to REALLY Pay "Wholesale" for College
Andrew Lockwood, CollegeSuccessBulletin.com

CHAPTER 27

DIVORCED AND SEPARATED FAMILIES
When "Mr. Wrong" can turn into "Mr. Right"

Many parents from divorced families make a mistake on the financial aid forms. They assume that, if they declare the child as a dependent for tax purposes, that means that they are the "custodial" parent for FAFSA purposes, and must file the FAFSA for their child.

But it ain't necessarily so. FAFSA cares about the parent with whom the child spends the majority of his/her time – anything over 50%. (Duh.)

In many divorces, the parents alternate who declares the child as a dependent, each year, thus claiming the deduction and lowering their tax bills. I think the FAFSA rules recognize this.

I have a client, Gary, who's self-employed – he runs a couple of dance studios. He shows hardly any money (profits) on paper, in fact, he filed bankruptcy a few years ago.

Gary's college-aged two kids split their time between him and his ex-wife. His ex is a physical therapist, who earns a nice salary. She filed the FAFSA for each of their two children.

Big mistake – the family would have tripled their eligibility if Gary were the "nominee" on the FAFSA – he shows hardly any income.

What if your child spends more time with the high-earning, divorced parent? Maybe you re-think these living arrangements for financial aid purposes. Don't do anything unethical, but remember, the standard you must meet is that the child must spend "most" of his/her time with the custodial parent. Most means 50.000000001% in the Base Year (defined earlier).

I had a client, Marc, a couple of years ago who, according to his financial aid forms, resided with his self-employed father on the South Shore of Long Island. Yet, somehow he attended high school 20 miles away on the North Shore, where his mother lived, coincidentally![83]

He cleaned up financial aid-wise at George Washington. And the following year, he did really well, academically. So well that he applied to transfer to Georgetown, and got in!

But there was an issue. Georgetown looks at the financials of both the custodial and non-custodial parent. Marc's award from

---

[83] Weasel disclaimer: this is not advice. Don't do anything unethical. I'm merely relaying facts. - Andy "Still a Recovering Attorney" Lockwood.

How to REALLY Pay "Wholesale" for College
Andrew Lockwood, CollegeSuccessBulletin.com

Georgetown was much worse than GW's, who only looks at one parent's info. He stayed at GW.

Another common question: what if a divorced parent remarries?

FAFSA counts "Household Income," meaning the new husband or wife's finances ARE part of the equation. Even if New Hubby has no legal or ethical obligation to support the college-bound kid from the divorced family.

However, financial aid officers have "Professional Discretion" to consider any and all non-formulaic factors, so they will adjust an Expected Family Contribution on occasion, including for situations like this. Sometimes.

Let me round out this discussion by addressing the CSS Profile, the form used by approximately 200, mostly private colleges (including GW and Georgetown, Marc's colleges). Many, but not all, CSS Profile colleges require information about the non-custodial parent. So this potential loophole may not work for this batch of schools. Here's a link to the NCP:

https://ncprofile.collegeboard.com/ncpWeb/pageflows/Main/NcpMainController.jpf

Another common question divorced parents ask (always moms): "What if my ex won't contribute a nickel toward college? Do I still need to force him to fill out the Non-Custodial Profile?"

Ah, the Deadbeat Dad.[84] I do not have a perfect answer to this question, other than you should inform the financial aid office if this is your reality. Many schools recognize that ex-spouses can be extremely uncooperative and will consider that when awarding financial aid.

But not all will believe you. Some (like BU, in my experience) will take the approach that it's not their problem that Deadbeat Dad won't cooperate. They'll either refuse to consider the financial aid application at all, or they'll assign an arbitrary Expected Family Contribution to DD.

If you're divorced, I'm sure you have your own definition of what constitutes the "wrong" parent. But in financial aid, you'd be well served to choose the "right" parent!

---

[84] Never a Deadbeat Mom...sigh...

CHAPTER 28

How Is Money Awarded?
What does a financial aid package look like – loans, scholarships, what?

What is "financial aid?" Is it all loans?

Financial aid is an umbrella term. It means free money – grants and scholarships – and "self-help" – loans and work study.

Different colleges dole out awards in different ways. The more elite colleges with larger endowments tend to award 80% and up in free stuff, while the land-grant, public universities might award packages 50% grants/scholarships, 50% loans/works study.

Let's look at this stuff one-by-one.

Although "Financial Aid" means only three things: loans, work-study and "free stuff" (grants, scholarships.), the total amount of aid, and HOW it's awarded, varies greatly by college.

A perplexing issue is that, especially when it comes to loans, colleges use different terms (pun intended)[85] .

---

[85] Loans have terms - the length of time you repay them...never mind.

How to REALLY Pay "Wholesale" for College
Andrew Lockwood, CollegeSuccessBulletin.com

So a Stafford Subsidized Loan is the same as the Direct Subsidized Loan.

Ditto for the Stafford Unsubsidized Loan and the Direct Unsubsidized Loan.

Some colleges "award" you a Parent Loan (PLUS), but this product is a federally mandated "gap filler" designed to help you pay the difference between 1. The total Cost of Attendance at the college, and 2. The amount of financial aid received. In other words, the financial aid office is not giving it to the student, the Department of Education is offering it to the parent. (I break down the different kinds of loans in the next chapter.)

RE: student loans: There are safeguards in place, the college must certify to a lender that the child is enrolled. Many colleges are now requiring loan counseling before they allow the student to take the funds.

Much of the communication from a financial aid office or lender goes to the student, not the parent. Make sure your child knows this and checks his email regularly. (As I was writing another part of this book, I got an email from a kid, panicking, because he hadn't received his loan paperwork from the school. Turns out that it was sitting in his email from five weeks ago.)

Or see if the financial aid office will cc you on these communications. They do this sometimes.

CHAPTER 29

AVOID DEADLY STUDENT LOAN TRAPS

This chapter makes my stomach turn. It's by far the most painful part of this book for me to write, because of my own depressing, horrible experience with student loans. Between college and law school, I capped out at close to $100,000.

Actually, it was more, but I paid of my undergrad loans before I went to law school, by bartending two-three jobs, working seven days per week (it was really fun, I'm not complaining at all. Truthfully, it was a little too fun, but the party had to end sometime.)

I never had a clue about loans. I wish my parents had given me a message other than, "Don't worry, it will all work out."

I don't fault them because of their backgrounds, but they sure were wrong – it definitely did NOT work out – I couldn't make the payments. I had all sorts of stress and credit issues, some which still crop up unexpectedly, all the bad stuff that happens to people who get in over their heads financially.

My hope for writing this book – and for being in the college consulting business, for that matter – is to help anyone I can avoid what I went through.

Let's start with the basics.

For more than two years, experts have predicted that student lending is poised to be the next "bubble."

And for good reason – student debt passed consumer debt as the largest category of money owed by Americans – going past the 1 Trillion mark in 2010. Defaults are on the rise. Young, entrepreneurial-minded college graduates cite loan payments as the main factor preventing them from starting up a company.

If innovation slows, the long-term effects of the student loan problem could be a lot worse than a bubble.

According to The Project on Student Debt, the average college student graduates with $24,000 in loans. And there are plenty of horror stories of couples trying to start a family saddled with $250,000 between them – having financed two undergraduate and one postgraduate education, for example.

The reason the pundits point to this as a potential bubble is commonsensical – the confluence of debt at all-time high, combined with arguably the worst job market for college graduates ever.

How to REALLY Pay "Wholesale" for College
Andrew Lockwood, CollegeSuccessBulletin.com

It's not easy to make payments of $750 per month when you have no income and no prospects around the corner.

Here's a rundown of the most common types of college loans.

The Stafford (or "Direct") subsidized loan

The Stafford (or "Direct") unsubsidized loan[86]

The PLUS Loan (Parent Loan for Undergraduate Students)

Private student loans

Note: In Summer 2013, Congress approved a law which changed student loans. Rates are lower now, but as the 10 Year Treasury Note goes higher, so will college loan rates, because loans now adjust each year (their rates were fixed before). Here are the most common types of loans.

Stafford Loan – Subsidized

These are the most benign of all the loan options available for a few reasons:

The interest rates are relatively low - 3.4%

The government pays ("subsidizes") the interest rate until six months after graduation

---

[86] I'm going to call each of them "Stafford" instead of saying "Stafford or Direct" each time. I think you would have figured this out, but there's always one or two sticklers who would point this out if I didn't say this. Geez.

137
How to REALLY Pay "Wholesale" for College
Andrew Lockwood, CollegeSuccessBulletin.com

Fees are non-existent (practically)

The amounts you can borrow don't go very far (up to $5,500, usually $3,500 is the maximum)

Students used to apply to third parties for Stafford loans, like banks and other lenders. Now, by going directly to the colleges, students pay lower fees.

Unsubsidized Stafford Loan.

The key differences between the Subsidized and Unsubsidized Stafford Loans are:

The interest on the Unsubsidized Stafford accrues immediately (the government doesn't "subsidize" it)

The interest on the Unsubsidized Stafford resets every year, it's fixed on the Subsidized Stafford. (The rate for the Unsubsidized Stafford was briefly 6.8%, until Congress lowered it to 3.4%). The rate is capped at 8.25%.

Combined annual loan limits for each type of Stafford start at $5,500 for freshmen, then increase to $6,500 for sophomores, then $7,500 per year for each remaining year of college.

Perkins Loan

This is primarily for low income families. The interest rate is low (5%), so are the loan amounts –typically $1,000 or so. I don't see a lot of these in my practice, but they are great loans (which is hard for me to say).

Here's a great, clear site that explains all this loan stuff, plus a lot of the boring nitty-gritty details I don't want to get bogged down with:

http://www.finaid.org/loans/studentloan.phtml

(See this site for more details – like how to apply, how to fill out the Master Promissory Note and other information. Also check out www.StudentLoans.gov - the official site of the Department of Education – for the rest of the story.)

Now let's look at the PLUS loan, one of the worst names in the history of financial products. It's a big negative for parents.

How to REALLY Pay "Wholesale" for College
Andrew Lockwood, CollegeSuccessBulletin.com

How to REALLY Pay "Wholesale" for College
Andrew Lockwood, CollegeSuccessBulletin.com

CHAPTER 30

THE PLUS LOAN

A Subprime Loan from Uncle Sam

Here are the facts on the PLUS Loan:

It is offered by the financial aid office to parents – but it is NOT financial aid – it's a loan product to fill the "gap" between the college's financial aid award to you and the amount you have to cough up.

It currently carries an interest rate of 6.41%, adjusts like the Unsubsidized Stafford and is capped at 10.5%.

It's payable over 10 years – making the payments higher than a 30 year mortgage, for example.

Here's the worst part about the PLUS loan – The Department of Education charges a 4% origination fee on this loan – so if you need to net $100,000, you'll borrow $104,000!

(I read that the government made something like $55 Billion in profits from lending to students and parents last year, which is more than the earnings of Exxon Mobile – the most profitable company in the world, and several of the country's biggest companies combined!)

To be eligible for a PLUS loan:

You must be the biological or adoptive parent of the student;

The student must be a dependent (under age 24) enrolled at least half-time;

You must pass a credit check (less rigorous than applying for a mortgage, though); and

You must apply with a Master Promissory Note (MPN in financial aid lingo).

The limit is the college's Cost of Attendance less any financial aid it has awarded (that's the "gap" I mentioned before)

Of course this is only a summary. Here's the Department of Education's link for the PLUS loan:

http://studentaid.ed.gov/PORTALSWebApp/students/english/parentloans.jsp

CHAPTER 31

PRIVATE STUDENT LOANS
Not quite as sucky as you'd think (but still pretty ugly)

Thanks to our financial meltdown in 2008, there are a LOT fewer choices of private student lenders than before (banks and other lenders that finance college, not the government).

The Consumer Financial Protection Bureau estimated that there are $165 billion in private loans (compared to 1.2 trillion in federal student loans).

Until the law changed in summer 2013, I thought of private student loans as a last resort. And they still are, for many people, because they are generally high rate (frequently double-digit), high fee, variable – not fixed – instruments.

But I've noticed that some lenders don't charge anywhere near the 4% origination fee that the Department of Education dings you for on the PLUS loan. Many don't charge at all.

How to REALLY Pay "Wholesale" for College
Andrew Lockwood, CollegeSuccessBulletin.com

And, now that the PLUS loan is variable, some private loans don't look as bad as they used to - if only by comparison. The old hierarchy of financial aid used to be:

Grants and Scholarships

Work Study/outside employment

Stafford Subsidized Loans/Perkins Loans

Stafford Unsubsidized Loans

Home Equity/Mortgage Loans

Parent Loans (PLUS)

Robbing a bank

Private Student Loans

Now, I'd flip-flop Private Student Loans and the PLUS loan on a case-by-case basis.

Here are some key concepts you should know about private student loans.

APR

Interest rates are important. But APR – Annualized Percentage Rate – is more important. APR is a formulaic representation of the true cost of your credit – interest rates AND fees – that was designed to allow you to make an apples to apples comparison between loan offers (whether mortgage loans, auto

How to REALLY Pay "Wholesale" for College
Andrew Lockwood, CollegeSuccessBulletin.com

loans or student loans). Because a lender can '"tease" you with a lower rate but bury fees in the mountains of disclosures you sign, APR is designed to make this process more "transparent" as the attorneys and regulators say.

You won't know your actual interest rate (and APR) until your loan application has cleared underwriting – meaning they've looked at your credit score, income, other debts, whether you floss regularly and if you're good to your mother. So don't assume an advertised rate is the rate you'll be approved for - it's designed to get you to apply.

How Rates Adjust

These interest rates are almost always variable rates, meaning they adjust at certain junctures.   Here is how many of them are calculated (this is complicated but important to understand):

INDEX + MARGIN = RATE

"Index" refers to a benchmark, or measurement like LIBOR – a rate set by European banks that is similar to the Prime Rate. This is also the cost of money to the student lender.

"Margin" means the spread that gets added to the Index. This is where the lenders make a profit (a synonym for "Margin").

So let's say that this index – LIBOR – is currently .5% and the margin is 7, your rate is 7.5%.(Index + Margin).

The better your credit history, the lower the perceived risk to the lender – and the lower your margin. Your interest rate and APR should be lower. You'll pay less.

If you have some dings on your credit, your margin, and interest rate will be higher, because you represent a higher risk.

Co-signing

If you must co-sign for your child (almost always required), check if the terms allow you to be dropped as a guarantor after a certain history of on-time payments – typically two years.

Look at the flexibility of payment terms – some loans allow you to defer payments until after you graduate, some require payments even though your child is in college.

Ask for discounts – sometimes student lenders will lower the interest rate if you sign up for auto-debits that come right out of your checking account – probably around ¼ of 1%. I'm not a big fan of this but you may be more comfortable with giving access to your bank account!

Be wary of college "Preferred Lender Lists." Although not as common as a couple of years ago, many colleges would publish a list of four-10 lenders on their site as "Preferred Lenders." Now, I hope you're sitting down before I lay this one on you....these

How to REALLY Pay "Wholesale" for College
Andrew Lockwood, CollegeSuccessBulletin.com

colleges would get "referral fees"[87] for sending applicants to the lenders on the Preferred Lender list! So just because a college "prefers" a lender does not mean that you should.

Here is an objective listing, alphabetically, of student lenders right from the Finaid.org website:

http://www.finaid.org/loans/privatestudentloans.phtml

New Yorkers would be well-served to noodle around on the Higher Education Services Corporation (HESC) website to compare student loan terms – here's the link:

https://www.hescmarketplace.org/marketplace/jsp/main/index.jsp

Connecticut and many other states have equivalent, low interest loan offerings. Check out your home state student lending websites.

---

[87] "Kick back" is such a vulgar term.

CHAPTER 32

How Much Money Do Grads of Elite Colleges Make?

According to a recent New York Times article, graduates of the most selective colleges earned more than 40% per year than those who graduated from the least selective schools. But, like any statistic, there's more than meets the eye.

Think about it: wouldn't you assume that the hardest working, most motivated kids would tend to apply to the toughest schools to get into? They could be successful no matter where they went. There's got to be a big element of self-selection in that stat..

Anyhoo, check out this list of colleges, ranked by alumni salary on Payscale.com:

Princeton University

Harvey Mudd College

California Institute of Technology (Caltech)

United States Naval Academy (USNA) at Annapolis

How to REALLY Pay "Wholesale" for College
Andrew Lockwood, CollegeSuccessBulletin.com

United States Military Academy (USMA) at West Point

Massachusetts Institute of Technology (MIT)

Lehigh University

Polytechnic Institute of New York University (NYU-Poly)

Babson College

Stanford University

Williams College

Stevens Institute of Technology

University of Notre Dame

Harvard University

Dartmouth College

Colgate University

SUNY Maritime College

Brown University

Santa Clara University

Washington and Lee University

College of the Holy Cross

Source: http://www.payscale.com/college-salary-report-2013/full-list-of-schools

CHAPTER 33

THE CHAPTER ABOUT ROI

Another fun, interesting (to me, but I'm weird) list from PayScale.com – colleges with the best and worst Returns on Investment (over 30 years)!

Again, there's always a back story behind any statistic, but this list shows that there are plenty of colleges that are worth considering, even though they may be off your radar.

Among the best:

>SUNY Maritime (surprise!)

>Colorado School of Mines (yes!)

>MIT (no surprise)

>Caltech

>Harvey Mudd (#1)

Among the worst: a bunch of art schools.

No shinola!

Check out these lists: http://www.payscale.com/college-education-value-2013

One parting, odd comment (from a college consultant): I don't think every kid should go to college! At least not right away.

I'm a big fan of the "Gap Year" (a year off between high school and college). I remember my Dad suggesting it to me. My response: "Are you stupid? None of my friends are doing that."

I would have benefitted from this advice.

I think it's fair to look at alternatives to college, too. Check out James Altucher's thoughts about other things to do:

http://www.jamesaltucher.com/2012/04/new-book-40-alternatives-to-college/

I found myself nodding in agreement after almost every sentence. Read it!

CHAPTER 34

ENTREPRENEURIAL CHILD?

A lot of my clients (almost 40%) are business owners, we talk a lot about business crap, all the time. Check out these top entrepreneurial colleges, ranked by *Entrepreneur Magazine*. (I've never taken a course on "entrepreneurialism," so I can't speculate what these schools teach. I struggle with the inherent conflict between academic and street smarts.)

You might be surprised at the lack of "brand name" colleges on this list – here's a sample:

Babson

Baylor

University of Houston

USC

Wash U

Brigham Young

U of Arizona

Temple

UNC

U of Oklahoma

Source:

http://www.entrepreneur.com/topcolleges/undergrad/0.html

Their list of top entrepreneurial grad schools contains a
couple of brand names but also some schools that will surprise you!

http://www.entrepreneur.com/topcolleges/grad/0.html

How to REALLY Pay "Wholesale" for College
Andrew Lockwood, CollegeSuccessBulletin.com

CHAPTER 35

GENEROUS SCHOOLS FOR B STUDENTS

I've gotten questions like "It seems like your advice is only for super high achieving kids. I have a "normal" child – will your stuff work for him?"

Most of my clients are in the B plus to A minus range. Maybe 10% or so are super high achievers, and 5% fall into the B to B minus or lower category.

Here's a great list – it comes from the website, DIYCollegeRankings.com (highly recommended). These schools each admit more than 50% of applicants and give grants to 97-100% of freshman, averaging $17,000 plus per:

Assumption College
Hood College
Albion College
College of Saint Benedict
Saint Johns University
Gustavus Adolphus College
Hamline University
William Jewell College
Millsaps College

How to REALLY Pay "Wholesale" for College
Andrew Lockwood, CollegeSuccessBulletin.com

Salem College
Creighton University
Colby-Sawyer College
Saint Anselm College
Elmira College
Clarkson University
Niagara University
Saint Bonaventure University
Wagner College
Canisius College
Xavier University
Ohio Wesleyan University
The College of Wooster
John Carroll University
Capital University
Wittenberg University
Pacific University
Saint Vincent College
Chatham University
Westminster College
Allegheny College
Lycoming College
Arcadia University
Juniata College
Ursinus College
The University of the Arts
La Salle University
Elizabethtown College
Susquehanna University
Erskine College and Seminary
Presbyterian College
Maryville College
University of Dallas
Austin College
Randolph College
Randolph-Macon College
Sweet Briar College
Hollins University

How to REALLY Pay "Wholesale" for College
Andrew Lockwood, CollegeSuccessBulletin.com

Bridgewater College
Hampden-Sydney College
Roanoke College
Saint Michael's College
Lawrence University
Beloit College
Wheeling Jesuit University

CHAPTER 36

THE 20 MOST EXPENSIVE COLLEGES

Look at college tuition numbers, and you might have a few reactions:

Jesus, I can't believe how much they charge!

Sweet mother of Jesus, those are TUITION-ONLY numbers – they don't include room and board?

Why are they all the same?

Here are the most expensive colleges, by tuition:

Columbia

Sarah Lawrence (!)

Vassar

George Washington

Trinity

Carnegie Mellon

Connecticut College

How to REALLY Pay "Wholesale" for College
Andrew Lockwood, CollegeSuccessBulletin.com

Wesleyan University (yay! My alma mater, somehow the third most expensive school in Connecticut, and somehow Yale isn't in the top two!)

Bucknell

Bard College at Simon's Rock (What? Do you know anyone who went here?)

Most of the colleges on this list offer hefty tuition discounts (duh – the point of this book).

So let's look at the highest NET PRICES charged, and see if you can deduce a common trait shared by most of the top ones, "Columbo:"

School of the Art Institute of Chicago

Ringling College of Art and Design

The Boston Conservatory

Berklee College of the Arts

California Institute of the Arts

The New School

Art Center College of Design

San Francisco Art Institute

New York University (also on the highest tuition chart, which proves my point about NYU – they suck.)

So the most expensive colleges are performing arts schools! Nothing like earning your degree, racking up $200,0000 in debt,

How to REALLY Pay "Wholesale" for College
Andrew Lockwood, CollegeSuccessBulletin.com

then waiting tables and auditioning while you hope to somehow make your $700/month loan payments, right?

Source: http://collegecost.ed.gov/catc/#

How to REALLY Pay "Wholesale" for College
Andrew Lockwood, CollegeSuccessBulletin.com

CHAPTER 37

THE 20 MOST EXPENSIVE DORMS

The true cost of college is not just tuition, but other "stuff" too- like room and board. This list shows the most expensive dorms – sorry, "residences"[88] - in the country last year

College	Room/Board
1. The New School	$18,080
2. New York University	$15,181
3. Fordham University – Lincoln Center	$15,000
4. Fordham University – Rose Hill	$14,925
5. St. John's University (Queens)	$14,700
6. Suffolk University	$14,624
7. Manhattanville College	$14,520
8. Pace University	$14,230
9. University of California – Berkeley	$14,046
10. Marymount Manhattan College	$14,030
11. Franklin W. Olin College of Engineering	$14,000
12. Sarah Lawrence College	$13,958
13. Dominican University of California	$13,900
14. University of California – Santa Cruz	$13,869
15. Harvey Mudd College	$13,858

---

[88] I can't in good conscience call a suite with flat panel TVs and granite counters a "Dorm," can you?

How to REALLY Pay "Wholesale" for College
Andrew Lockwood, CollegeSuccessBulletin.com

16. Cooper Union for Advancement of Science $13,700
17. University of California – Santa Barbara $13,694
18. American University $13,684
19. Claremont McKenna College $13,625
20. Vanderbilt University $13,560

Source: http://www.campusgrotto.com/most-expensive-college-dorms-for-2011-2012.html

How to REALLY Pay "Wholesale" for College
Andrew Lockwood, CollegeSuccessBulletin.com

CHAPTER 38

KIPLINGER'S TOP 100 BEST VALUE PUBLIC SCHOOLS

Kiplinger's publishes interesting lists, too. Here are some highlights from their list of the 100 Best Value public universities.

The University of North Carolina at Chapel Hill

University of Virginia

University of Florida

College of William and Mary

University of Maryland

 UCLA

New College of Florida

Cal Berkeley

SUNY Geneseo

UC San Diego

How to REALLY Pay "Wholesale" for College
Andrew Lockwood, CollegeSuccessBulletin.com

Source: http://www.kiplinger.com/tool/college/T014-S001-kiplinger-s-best-values-in-public-colleges/index.php

How to REALLY Pay "Wholesale" for College
Andrew Lockwood, CollegeSuccessBulletin.com

CHAPTER 39

KIPLINGER'S BEST VALUES IN PRIVATE COLLEGES

Kiplinger's also publishes a list of best value private colleges, based on several factors including average grant per student, debt-load per graduate and four-year graduation rate and other factors.

Again, many usual suspect, schools:

Yale
Princeton
Duke
Harvard
But also some less-obvious choices:
Richmond
GW
Elon
Drake
Gonzaga
Clark
U Miami
All of these colleges cracked the top 50. Check out the whole list:

http://www.kiplinger.com/tool/college/T014-S001-kiplinger-s-best-values-in-private-colleges/index.php

How to REALLY Pay "Wholesale" for College
Andrew Lockwood, CollegeSuccessBulletin.com

How to REALLY Pay "Wholesale" for College
Andrew Lockwood, CollegeSuccessBulletin.com

CONCLUSION

Now you posses an arsenal of money-saving tips and strategies about how to play the financial aid game to win. You also know about a bunch of money-sucking "landmines" to avoid.

This book is general advice, and necessarily incomplete. I tried to make this book easy to read and use, as opposed to a dry, scholarly textbook that stinks to read...and write.

This information is just a starting point. The saying is "Knowledge is power," but I think that's misleading.

Knowledge is useless without IMPLEMENTATION! So here is a summary of what we covered, and some homework.

1. Research the historical generosity of every school on your list. Check out the Common Data Set, the College Board and the various and sundry Net Price Calculators.

2. Determine how they meet financial need – the percentage that's free and the amount that's loans/works study. Same resources.

How to REALLY Pay "Wholesale" for College
Andrew Lockwood, CollegeSuccessBulletin.com

3. Determine your EFC and how you can lower just by shifting your savings from non-exempt assets into exempt assets. See my blog - www.CollegePlanningGuru.com - for more examples (click on "events").

4. If you're going to "shelter" your assets, do it before your Base Year (the calendar year that ends in the middle of the year before you file your financial aid forms) [89] to avoid any impact on your tax returns that will be reviewed by the financial aid office. But be wary of the taxes you'll pay, the potential penalties, and the features of any exempt financial instrument you use to implement one of the strategies in this book or anything you stumble across.

5. Know your priority deadlines. Check out the website for EACH college on your list.

6. Even if you make seven figures, there's a lot of money available for you - apply to schools STRATEGICALLY, not only Rear Window Sticker Colleges.

7. Don't give up if you've received a lousy award – you might be able to improve it: AppealsClass.com

---

[89] There's GOT to be a better way to say this...If your kid graduates 2016, your base year is 2015. So try to confine any of your slick, wheeler-dealer moves to the 2014 tax year!

How to REALLY Pay "Wholesale" for College
Andrew Lockwood, CollegeSuccessBulletin.com

I hope you found this book to be valuable and that you feel better about tackling this overly-complicated, intimidating, high-stakes process!

Special offer from Moi to You

If, after you've diligently combed your way through this book, you still have questions about your own personal college financial plan, I'm happy to chat with you, no charge, for 20 minutes on the phone. (I bill at $450 per hour, and my fees typically range from $1,600 to more than $7,500, depending on how much time I work with the students, if I work with them at all).

www.CollegePlanningGuru.com – click on "contact."

Also, I encourage you to listen to *The College Success for Less Podcast,* available at www.CollegePlanningGuru.com – click on "podcast."

You can email me at andy@andylockwood.com, too. I want to hear about your successes!

Good luck!

About Andrew Lockwood

Andrew Lockwood is a controversial, outspoken (some say, "obnoxious") critic of runaway college costs and a college finance and admissions consultant. He specializes in helping "Forgotten Middle Class" families take advantage of legal and ethical loopholes in the federal financial aid system so that they can pay for a top college without filing bankruptcy.

Daily, Andy witnesses first-hand the stress and emotional roller coaster felt by parents of college-bound children caused by outrageous, skyrocketing bills from America's top colleges and wrote *How to Pay "Wholesale" for College* to help.

A highly sought after and entertaining (to himself) public speaker, Andy lectures several times a month on college finance's "secrets" at libraries and high schools, to PTA/PTO's, financial planners, numerous Temples, Jewish Community Centers, Adult Education Centers, and other civic and religious organizations. Andy hosted the radio show *"The College Planning Power Hour"* on ESPN radio in Ft. Lauderdale, Florida, and currently hosts and publishes the *College Success for Less* podcast, available on iTunes and Andy's website.

Andy chose his career because he personally amassed more than $100,000 in student debt between undergraduate studies at Wesleyan University, where he was a member[90] of the basketball team – and St. John's University School of Law. Now, he and his

---

[90] Note – "played" basketball would be artistic license.

How to REALLY Pay "Wholesale" for College
Andrew Lockwood, CollegeSuccessBulletin.com

wife, Pearl, have sworn a blood oath that they will never allow their four children to go through what he endured.

Before becoming an entrepreneur, Andy practiced corporate law, where he was responsible for closing transactions of $500,000,000 and up, served as in-house counsel to a publicly traded broker-dealer and as a member of the board of directors of a publicly-traded education company.

Andy is a member of the New York State Financial Aid Administrators' Association (NYSFAA) and the New York State Admissions Counselors Association (NYSAC). He writes the *Financial Aid "Secrets"* column the *NewsCaster,* the trade publication for the NYSAC.

A native of Newton, Massachusetts, Andy is a die-hard fan of the Red Sox, Celtics, Patriots and other teams hated by New Yorkers.

More information is available at CollegePlanningGuru.com.

Nice comments.

From the minute I walked in your door for the first time, I felt an enormous weight had been lifted off me. Thank you for all that you have done to help me and my precious girls.

- Beth Freeman
Scottsdale, Arizona

# # #

Just to let you know that I am spreading the word about Andy coming to GCHS in May and that many of our parents and students should attend. I was a fan but now I know how much work you guys do and how helpful it is. Well worth the money.

Mary Ellen Cuomo
Teacher, Key Club Advisor, Glen Cove High School
North Shore High School SEPTA Board Member

# # #

What more could you possibly ask for? Incredibly insightful and helpful advice delivered concisely and humorously. Andy Lockwood has the credentials, the experience, the wisdom, the strong work ethic and a true sense of honesty. As far as I'm concerned, if you want to pay less for college....read Andy's book....then call the guy. He's the same in person only taller.

Randy Levin – College Essay Specialist
www.WriteToCollege.com

# # #

Hi Andy,
Thank you for your guidebook. Normally I have to suffer through a variety of dry college guides and references in order to get updated information on the college and financial aid process. Your style of writing made it not only easy to read, but it made me laugh along the way. Not being an expert in the financial aid process, I felt your explanation provided a no-nonsense

breakdown on the best methods in planning to pay for college. During my college planning meetings, I feel comfortable recommending your book to my parents to assist in their financial planning.
Sincerely
Mike
Guidance Counselor
Long Island

# # #

Dear Andy,

I wanted to send you a letter thanking you for all of your help over the past few months. From the time I went to your seminar I felt so much more comfortable in what I had to do and how the whole process of applying for financial aid /scholarships worked.

It literally was a huge relief knowing that there was help out there and you guided us step by step. You saved me thousands of dollars that will enable me to lose a little less sleep.

Thanks for your help, guidance and for always being there when I had dozens of questions. The bad part for you is that with my two other children you will have to deal with me for the next 10 years, good luck with that.

Sincerely yours

Michael Levy
Roslyn, New York

# # #

I told them I don't want to play games with my money or get some extra bill in the future. They promised I would get back five times what I invested for the service.

They were true to their word.

Debbie & Terry Cooney
Davie, Florida

#

Dear Andy:

We wanted to let you know Clark selected Georgia Tech and is starting engineering school there in August.

Thank you so much for your support and guidance and expert advice during this collegiate process.

Peter Strugatz
Carrie Clark
Easthampton, New York

#

I came away from our meeting thinking, "How can I NOT afford to hire Andy!"

Ralph Rizzuto
Huntington, New York

#

Dear Andy,

I just wanted to thank you again for your help.

We knew that our financial situation was a little complicated to explain and so originally went to another college finance consultant for assistance. Despite his help, our application for aid was rejected and our joy at our son's acceptance to his school of first choice turned into panic. I didn't know how we could pay the full amount, over $60,000 per year, without jeopardizing our other children's educational options. It was about that time that I attended one of your free lectures and realized we might still have a chance. I was impressed with your clear, no nonsense approach and decided to try again.

You took considerable time going over all our financials and business history and then gave us excellent advice. Your quick grasp of the issues,

How to REALLY Pay "Wholesale" for College
Andrew Lockwood, CollegeSuccessBulletin.com

optimism, easy manner and expertise were reassuring and invaluable. Thanks to your efforts, we were able to receive the financial aid we needed, almost $15,000, even though we had already been turned down once before.

We're very grateful for your help and wouldn't hesitate for a minute to recommend you to our friends. I'm only sorry we didn't go to you first.

Sincere regards,

[Name withheld for publication out of paranoia that client's son's Ivy League college will discover this somehow and reduce his award]

# # #

My son was admitted to Tulane University and received an extremely generous aid package. I strongly believe that what I learned from you was a big part of it.

Mitchell Fein
Great Neck, New York

# # #

I met with you - you told me that you couldn't help me and not to waste my money. That's when I knew you were an honest guy!

Anthony DiBattista
New Hyde Park, NY

# # #

I don't know where to begin. Our financial aid packages are just now starting to come in and each one is better than the next. Just today Boston University gave is $40,000. Rob and I had no idea how were were possibly going to afford to send our girls to college. Thanks to your knowledge of filing and the FAFSA and CSS form, and your strategic positioning of our finances, we're now comfortable in knowing we are getting the most out of the system and will be able to put our girls through college. Thank you Andy! You made this process so easy and, dare I say,

How to REALLY Pay "Wholesale" for College
Andrew Lockwood, CollegeSuccessBulletin.com

downright fun...you helped us afford our kids' dream schools. Thank goodness you know all the loopholes.

Very truly yours,

Stephanie and Rob Salzbank
Port Washington, NY

#

My son is going to a top college (George Washington) on monies he received totally from Andy's involvement. He looked me in the eye and told me...'I get my clients five times the amount of their investment. HE WASN'T KIDDING!!! Best money I ever spent.

Scott Sanders
Long Beach, NY

#

Dear Andy

I finally have a moment to thank you for all your help this year. I know that my circumstances are unusual. You pushed me outside of my comfort zone in order to financially benefit. And it worked! If you weren't beside me cheering me on, I would not have had the courage to approach the financial aid department at Syracuse - twice! You have been great throughout this experience.

Thanks again,

Diane
Bellmore

#

Dear Andy,

I wanted to thank you for all the help you have given me regarding my son Robert's financial planning for college.

You were an enormous help when I had problems with the FAFSA and eventually the appeal to SUNY Albany.

Your professionalism and patience is what makes you and your business so successful.

I am going to recommend you to all my friends so they can put their mind at ease and not have to worry about undertaking this daunting process alone!

Sincerely,

Sabrina Ferrara
Hauppauge, NY

# # #

Andy Lockwood and Staff
Dear Mr. Lockwood,

I would like to thank Andy and his staff, and provide affirmation that Andy's program works and is proven to be successful. Entering into our journey regarding how we will possibly be able to fund an annual expense of $30K plus is an over whelming mental experience. The typical family needs guidance and direction from a qualified individual and Andy is the person to do just that. Andy provided mental relief and was able to provide a strategy when completing the necessary details for the FASA. Andy provided clear cut direction based on his knowledge and awareness of financial aid available to most families regardless of financial status. Andy personally engagement in the process regarding the submission of the documents to the educational institutions of choice and provided an estimate of financial aid so there that there was an expectation, which allows for a family to plan accordingly. Due to Andy's experience and knowledge regarding available financial aid, the process of developing a plan to support my son's financial needs for his college education was actual a pleasant experience and not one of hardship and despair.

Once again thanks, Andy to you and your staff and the continued support in making this process a rewarding experience.

We have recommended your firm to a number of our family friends and we are grateful that we were able to have the opportunity to work closely with you on this very important milestone in my son's next step in life.

Most Sincerely
Sean Cunningham
Belleville, NJ

# # #

Please express my gratitude to Andy. My son qualified for very generous financial aid packages so far from the colleges we heard from. We are very happy and pleased!

If he mails me his business cards when he mails me back my tax information We will give them out to a few people whom we know really will benefit from his services, or possibly sponsor a seminar if he is interested.

Thanks again
Darlene
Locust Valley

# # #

Andy,

We want to thank you and Pearl for all your hard work handling our daughter's financial aid forms and advising us on the issues surrounding college admission. You simplified an often complex process and took a huge load off of our shoulders. While we should have listened to your advice regarding early decision, we were pleased with the increase in financial aid afforded to us. We look forward to your counsel in the years ahead for all three of our college bound children. It's great working with you both.

Jeanne & Gary Lofgren
Westbury, NY

# # #

The Weston High School PTO hosted Andy for an extremely informative and entertaining seminar on the best-kept secrets of securing the ideal financial aid package.

Weston is home to a high income parent population and most walked away not just pleased but astonished that they could, in fact, qualify for financial aid!

The PTO received terrific feedback and we are looking forward to having Andy back next year -- kudos to Andy for a job well done!

Lisa Bigelow
Vice President, Weston (Connecticut) High School PTO

# # #

I saw Andy's ad I was impressed with his knowledge of the whole financial aid process and very happy with the service he provides.

Initially, I thought I was just going to get financial aid advice but Andy helped us with a lot more than that. He spoke about camps Alexis should attend to showcase her talents, the sports resume to send out to colleges, sports DVD, the essays she should be writing, internships and just so many other little details that I just didn't think about. His rolodex is filled with the right connections that Lexi needed for the college process. He helped us market our daughter.

I think it would be worth your time to meet with Andy.

Thank you,

Karen Greene
Glen Head, New York

# # #

I met with my Teen Advisory Group on Tuesday and they told me they really enjoyed your presentation especially that you geared it for "the forgotten middle class", and gave them tips and information that they could *easily understand. They also liked your sense of humor and jokes and thought they enhanced an already fine presentation.*

Just wanted to let you know that I have you scheduled for a "College Finance Secrets" program...We are looking forward to your program, and I will be in touch a few weeks beforehand.
Sincerely,
Cathy Loechner,
Young Adult Librarian
Shelter Rock Public Library
516-248-7363 ext. 239

# # #

Lisa, Please thank Andy Lockwood for his wonderful presentation at our recent Board Meeting. We found it very informative and helpful.

I am sure a lot of the parents who attended the presentation will be following up with him for subsequent meetings.

Thanks again,
Lisa Edelblum
President, Roslyn High School Parent Faculty Association

# # #

Mr. Lockwood has presented several informative workshops at The Bryant Library in Roslyn over the past few years. Despite the dry subject matter of the college financial aid process, Mr. Lockwood engages the audience with both humor and honesty. His knowledge on an often confusing subject is evident during his workshop and parents are often eager to learn more from Mr. Lockwood.

Lauren Fazio -
Young Adult Librarian
The Bryant Library (Roslyn NY)

# # #

My library page told me her dad attended and said you were very good, better than the guy that had come here last year, {local business man). I also just got off the phone with a parent that called and thanked me for running your program. She said she and the other parents got a lot of good information and that you were a wonderful speaker and very animated. I told her I would make an effort to have you come back in the spring!

High marks indeed!

Thank you again!

Linda Meglio
Young Adult Librarian
Greenlawn Public Library

...My daughter's long and incongruent "wish list" quickly evolved into ten schools -three in-state and seven out of state , two back ups," the core choices and one stretch school. She was confident and focused as she plunged into the applications. With your guidance, she wrote some terrific essays and completed all ten on time. While all of this was going on you magically expedited the FAFSA and other financial paperwork to all the schools taking that burden and administrative nightmare off our shoulders.

The proof of your program was she was accepted at seven Top 100 schools four of which were out of state, waitlisted at two out of states and was only declined at the "stretch" school, Georgetown. As it turned out, the first school to reply was the one she finally chose but that was only decided once we had all the offers in hand. Every single school made very generous scholarship offers and we ended up choosing a Top 30 school that offered 95% of the total cost of attendance, 70% of which was free money!

We look forward to the next 4 years and our next child knowing that we have the College Planners on our team. Thanks again, Andy and Pete - it has been a pleasure working with you.

Regards,
Tom Browne
Weston, Florida

How to REALLY Pay "Wholesale" for College
Andrew Lockwood, CollegeSuccessBulletin.com

# # #

"The only thing trickier than applying to college is paying for it. That's why "Never Pay Retail for College" is so valuable. It takes readers through strategies they won't find elsewhere to reduce the burden of paying the pipers at America's colleges and universities. This book will pay for itself, many times over, and should be on the hard drive of any parents with college-bound kids."

– Matt Rees, Editor, FT Newsmine – a Financial Times publication, former Speechwriter for the Executive Office of the President, The Securities and Exchange Commission and the Secretary of the Treasury, Writer for The Wall Street Journal, The New York Times, The Economist and The Washington Post.

# # #

Families are faced with two very challenging hurdles as the first decade of the 21st Century nears a close: Where they can gain perspective and education on how to retire in the style they desire, and how to give their children the best chance to survive their own generation's financial challenges. It starts with a solid education. This book, by clearly defining the challenges and presenting some of the opportunities for those families, starts them on the road to addressing the latter challenge. By doing so, it may just help them move closer to achieving the former as well.

– Robert Isbitts, Author of "Wall Street Bull and How to Bear It", Chief Investment Officer, Emerald Asset Advisors and Worth Magazine's Top 100 Wealth Advisors

# # #

Like all parts of personal finance paying for college is becoming increasingly complex. Colleges are businesses that go through ups and downs like any other business. With endowments from private schools posting record breaking declines and 48 out of 50 states currently confronting budget deficits the costs for both private and public colleges are likely to keep going up at a rate faster than inflation.

Every parent regardless of income level should be going after financial aid and Never Pay Retail For College is exactly the tool to help people learn the strategic ins and outs of every aspect of planning, applying and negotiating for college aid. There are 70 factors that go into determining aid packages, can you even name four? Never Pay Retail For College also debunks numerous myths about college like private school potentially being cheaper than public schools. Maybe you don't know how that can be but the authors of Never Pay Retail For College do.

– Roger Nussbaum, Chief Investment Officer, Your Source Financial, Phoenix, Arizona, (commentator on CNBC – Asia, publisher of RandomRoger.com)

Dear Mr. Lockwood

I am writing this letter to recommend your services to any parent that has a son or daughter approaching college. We received guidance for career choices, college selection and obtained financial aid advice from College Planning Specialists.

The financial aid award we received was much greater than we had envisioned.

Mr. Lockwood is knowledgeable, professional and very accommodating to work with.

Please consult with him

Very truly yours,

Douglas P. Johnson
Attorney–at–law
Davie, Florida

Hello Andy,

How are you doing? I have some good news!!! U Miami's Office of Financial aid finally revised Farley's fafsa and financial aid package and gave us more money. I went from receiving 4,600 to receiving 13,730 and they also sent 4,000 back to my sallie mae loan. I'm so happy!! Thank you soo much!!!

Filberta LeTang

Miami, Florida

# # #

Dear College Pete and Andy:

We wanted to express our thanks and gratitude for your professional guidance in the college financial planning process. We first met with you at one of your seminars when Lauren was in the beginning of 10th grade. While initially it seemed perhaps to be a bit premature to plan for college three years in advance, it became clear that in fact that was the perfect time to start planning. You never made any guarantees other than that if we followed your strategies we would put ourselves in the best possible position to be eligible for financial assistance.

We had saved some money for college and had participated in the Florida Prepaid Plan, however we knew that if Lauren chose to go to a private university those funds would be grossly inadequate. Over the course of the next two and one half years we met with you from time to time to map out and plan the best strategy, so when the time came to apply for financial aid, we would be ready.

It became clear that Lauren wanted to go to a private school and in fact her top choice was Vanderbilt University. A prestigious school with a lofty sticker price ($58,000+). The good news was that Vanderbilt stated that they will meet 100% of the demonstrated need. With that in mind, and with your financial strategies in hand, we felt confident that Lauren would be eligible for a significant financial aid award. We felt so confident of this that we allowed Lauren to apply to Vanderbilt early decision. It should be noted that Pete mentioned more than once, that applying early decision might be statistically favorable in terms of admission, but could reduce our ability to negotiate financial aid if our initial award was low. (Smells like a disclaimer from College Pete).

Lauren received a letter from Vanderbilt approximately one month ago. The good news for her was that she was accepted for admission. This wonderful news was tempered by the fact that Vanderbilt's initial award for financial aid was approximately $9,000. Although $9,000 is nice, it clearly was significantly less than what we were expecting. Over the next week, I

How to REALLY Pay "Wholesale" for College
Andrew Lockwood, CollegeSuccessBulletin.com

followed Pete's advice on how to approach Vanderbilt's financial aid office and immediately contacted them to receive clarification on what the basis of the "low" award was. It became clear that Vanderbilt misconstrued some information on our tax return, and Pete, my accountant, and I worked closely together to further explain the tax situation. Ultimately, through perseverance and continued support from Pete the initial award was increased from $9,000.00 to $39,000. We are thrilled as parents as is our daughter, Lauren.

We would highly recommend your professional service to any family who is considering sending their child to a private university.

David and Lisa Reiser

# # #

Thank you for your guidance during this process. You and Pearl made it very easy.

Alan Karul
Plainview, New York

# # #

Thanks again for all your help - whenever I have a chance to speak to friends who have children with college ahead I recommend your services.

Regards,
Frank Brecher
Commack, New York

# # #

David was accepted at his first-choice school and we did indeed receive a very generous aid award, with no student loans required first year.

Thanks for your advice and for the information we received through your counseling, your book and the various online resources.

John Rivior
Huntington Station

New York

# # #

Hi Andy:

Two things that I have learned over the years:

1.   Hiring a specialist to assist you in navigating stuff you are not an expert in (you are a specialist as am I. I am coming to you for your expertise in the arena of colleges - you do that every day, you are an expert. Companies come to me to place their catastrophic risks- where I am an expert). I apply this in my business and personal life.

2.   Referral Business is my lifeline. If I do a good job for one guy he tells someone else. My best new business sources are from referrals and people who have done business with me in the past. So yes, if you do a good job for me I will brag to my friends about it.

I will admit that I was a little skeptical at first but awfully glad that we engaged your services I know that we have a ways to go but the first blush looks really great. [EDITOR'S NOTE: Kelly received an $96,000 scholarship offer from one of her two top choice schools.]

I sincerely appreciate you engaging Kelly, I wanted her to be the one to take the lead and responsibility for her own destiny. Having her accountable to someone else besides her Mom (and Dad) was a motivating factor. She was happy to have completed her essay over the summer and gotten an early leg up on the application process. Some of her friends have not even completed essays yet never mind applying to colleges.

Have a great Thanksgiving you and Pearl and the kids!

Theresa Lally
Syosset, New York

# # #

Made in the USA
Lexington, KY
30 August 2014